CHINESE HOROSCOPE 2024

Year of the Wooden Dragon

From February 10, 2024, to January 28, 2025

Angeline Rubi and Alina A. Rubi

Published Independently

Author: Angeline. Rubi and Alina A. Rubi

Email: rubiediciones29@gmail.com

Editing: Angeline Rubi

rubiediciones29@gmail.com

Introduction

The Chinese calendar is ancient and complex and has never been simplified. Many cultures replaced the Lunar calendar with the Sun calendar.

The Chinese, Islamic and Hebrew calendars are governed by the lunar phases. It is a complicated system since they are not only governed by lunar cycles, but also include the solar cycle, the cycle of Jupiter and Saturn.

The Chinese consider universal energy to be governed by balance. The concept of Yin and Yang is the most important within that balance. Yin is the opposite of Yang and vice versa, but together they achieve total balance. This energy can be found in everything that exists, the tangible and the intangible.

The Ying/Yang symbol is divided into two halves, one is black (Yin) and the other white (Yang). Both parts are joined in the middle by an ellipse that links them together to form a curve. Their colors, black and white, signify that duality exists, and that for one to exist, the other must undeniably exist. Inside the Yin there is a Yang circle, which symbolizes that darkness always requires light. Within the Yang we find a Yin circle, indicating that within the light we will always find darkness.

The ellipse that unites them means that everything flows, transforms, and evolves. If there is an imbalance of either of these two energies,

Yin or Yang, our life is not balanced, since together they strengthen each other. We should never think that one energy is superior to the other, both must concur equally.

Unfortunately, in our society there is a tendency to favor Yang energy, thinking that its characteristics are the most significant. By doing this we create a division between the spiritual and material plane, because by reducing the value of Yin energy we are less reflective, thinking that susceptibility is something negative, because it implies fragility.

The same thing happens with darkness, we not only avoid it, but we are afraid of it. Both energies are important. We can only be spiritual beings when there is a balance between Yin and Yang because you are not only light, but also dark. It is a mistake to value and privilege the strong, or action. We must appreciate and value the feminine, and sensitivity, because only in this way we can reach the true balance of our being, from a position of love and firmness.

In the signs of the Chinese zodiac are present the Yin and Yang energy, and they are the ones that will stipulate the characteristics of each animal, and the elements associated with them.

Yin energy is linked to the dark, cold, feminine, abstraction, the deep and the Moon. Yin signs are thoughtful, sensitive, and curious. They are the Ox, Rabbit, Snake, Goat, Rooster, and Pig.

Yang energy is related to light, warmth, superficiality, the Sun, and logical thinking. They are impulsive, and materialistic signs. They are Rat, Tiger, Dragon, Horse, Monkey and Dog.

The Yin and Yang energies are related to the elements, which in turn will be derived from the years in which they occur. Each element possesses Yin and Yang energy.

- The years ending in the number **0** have the element Metal and are related to Yang energy.
- The years ending in the number **1** have the element Metal and are related to Yin energy.
- Years ending in the number **2** have the element of Water and are related to Yang energy.

- Years ending in the number **3** have the element of Water and are related to Yin energy.
- The years ending in the number **4** have the element of Wood and are related to Yang energy.
- Years ending in the number **5** have the element of Wood and are related to Yin energy.
- The years ending in the number **6** have the element of Fire and are related to Yang energy.
- Years ending in the number **7** have the element of Fire and are related to Yin energy.
- The years ending in the number 8 have the element of Earth and are related to Yang energy.
- The years ending in the number **9** have the element of Earth and are related to Yin energy.

Origin of the Chinese Horoscope

The Chinese horoscope is a tradition of more than 5000 years and is based on lunar years.

Legend has it that Buddha called all the animals, however, only twelve attended his summons in the following order: the Rat, the Ox, the Tiger, the Rabbit, the Dragon, the Snake, the Horse, the Goat, the Monkey, the Rooster, the Dog, and the Pig.

Each animal received a year as a gift, forming the twelve-year cycle used in Chinese astrology. Therefore, each sign has a name of an animal, and to each animal corresponds a year.

Each animal was also assigned one of the five elements that correspond to the planetary energies:

- water (Mercury)
- metal (Venus)
- fire (Mars)
- wood (Jupiter)
- earth (Saturn)

The Chinese Horoscope expresses the analogy of cosmic energies with everyone. For that reason, the energy of each person is represented by one of the twelve animals that form this zodiacal system.

Each animal and the energy that corresponds to you is determined by your date of birth. These energies define your behaviors, and how you perceive the world. For the Chinese, these signs symbolize the most remarkable particularities of our character. To properly understand the meaning of animals we must see them as spiritual symbols.

The Chinese Horoscope is not based on the solar cycle, on which the western horoscope is based. It is based on the cycles of the Moon. Each lunar year has twelve new moons and every twelve years a thirteenth, therefore, a new year never coincides with the date of the previous year.

The twelve animals of the Chinese horoscope influence the life, luck and will of all human beings. These qualities do not manifest themselves openly in daily life, but they are always present, acting in the form of hidden forces.

The Chinese period of twelve years is linked to the transit of the planet Jupiter, and each Chinese lunar year in Western astrology corresponds to the duration of Jupiter's transit through a zodiac sign. Jupiter is always in the sign in Western astrology that traditionally corresponds to the animal in the Chinese horoscope.

Chinese Horoscope Years from 1960 to 2031

From 1960 to 1971

Year	Date	Animal and Element
1960	1960 January 28 - 1961 February 14	Metal Rat
1961	1961 February 15 - 1962 February 04	Metal Ox
1962	1962 February 05 - 1963 January 24	Water Tiger
1963	1963 January 25 - 1964 February 12	Water Rabbit
1964	1964 February 13 - 1965 February 01	Dragon Wood
1965	1965 February 02 - 1966 January 20	Snake Wood
1966	1966 January 21 - 1967 February 08	Fire Horse
1967	1967 January 09 - 1968 January 29	Fire Goat
1968	1968 January 30 - 1969 February 16	Earth Monkey
1969	1969 February 17 - 1970 February 05	Earth Horse
1970	1970 February 06 - 1971 January 26	Metal Dog
1971	1971 January 27 - 1972 February 14	Metal Pig

From 1972 to 1983

Year	Date	Animal and Element
1972	1972 February 15 - 1973 February 02	Water Rat
1973	1973 February 03 - 1974 January 22	Water Ox
1974	1974 January 23 - 1975 February 10	Wooden Tiger
1975	1975 February 11 - 1976 January 30	Wooden Rabbit
1976	1976 January 31 - 1977 February 17	Fire Dragon
1977	1977 February 18 - 1978 February 06	Snake Fire
1978	1978 February 07 - 1979 January 27	Earth Horse
1979	1979 January 28 - 1980 February 15	Earth Goat
1980	1980 February 16 - 1981 February 04	Metal Monkey
1981	1981 February 05 - 1982 January 24	Metal Horse
1982	1982 January 25 - 1983 February 12	Water Dog
1983	1983 February 13 - 1984 February 01	Water Pig

From 1984 to 1995

Year	Date	Animal and Element
1984	1984 February 02 - 1985 February 19	Wood Rat
1985	1985 February 20 - 1986 February 08	Wood Ox
1986	1986 February 09 - 1987 January 28	Fire Tiger
1987	1987 January 29 - 1988 February 16	Fire Rabbit
1988	1988 February 17 - 1989 February 05	Earth Dragon
1989	1989 February 06 - 1990 January 26	Earth Snake
1990	1990 January 27 - 1991 February 14	Metal Horse
1991	1991 February 15 - 1992 February 03	Metal Goat
1992	1992 February 04 - 1993 January 22	Water Monkey
1993	1993 January 23 - 1994 February 09	Water Rooster
1994	1994 February 10 - 1995 January 30	Wood Dog
1995	1995 January 31 - 1996 February 18	Wood Pig

From 1996 to 2007

Year	Date Animal and Element
1996	1996 February 19 - 1997 February 06 Fire Rat
1997	1997 February 07 - 1998 January 27 Fire Ox
1998	1998 January 28 - 1999 February 15 Earth Tiger
1999	1999 February 16 - 2000 February 04 Earth Rabbit
2000	2000 February 05 - 2001 January 23 Metal Dragon
2001	2001 January 24 - 2002 February 11 Metal Snake
2002	2002 February 12 - 2003 January 31 Water Horse
2003	2003 February 01 - 2004 January 21 Water Goat
2004	2004 January 22 - 2005 February 8 Wooden Monkey
2005	2005 February 9 - 2006 January 28 Wooden Rooster
2006	2006 January 29 - 2007 February 17 Fire Dog
2007	2007 February 18 - 2008 February 6 Fire Pig

From 2008 to 2019

Year	Date	Animal and Element
2008	2008 February 7 - 2009 January 25 Earth Rat
2009	2009 January 26 - 2010 February 13 Earth Ox
2010	2010 February 14 - 2011 February 2 Metal Tiger
2011	2011 February 3 - 2012 January 22 Metal Rabbit
2012	2012 January 23 - 2013 February 9 Water Dragon
2013	2013 February 10 - 2014 January 30 Water Snake
2014	2014 January 31 - 2015 February 18 Wood Horse
2015	2015 February 19 - 2016 February 7 Wood Goat
2016	2016 February 8 - 2017 January 27 Fire Monkey
2017	2017 January 28 - 2018 February 15 Fire Rooster
2018	2018 February 16 - 2019 February 4 Earth Dog
2019	2019 February 5 - 2020 January 24 Earth Pig

From 2020 to 2031

Year	Date	Animal and Element
2020	2020 January 25 - 2021 February 11 Metal Rat	
2021	2021 February 12 - 2022 January 31 Metal Ox	
2022	2022 February 1 - 2024 January 21 Water Tiger	
2024	2024 January 22 - 2024 February 9 Water Rabbit	
2024	2024 February 10 - 2025 January 28 Wood Dragon	
2025	2025 January 29- 2026 February 16 Wood Snake	
2026	2026 February 17 - 2027 February 5 Fire Horse	
2027	2027 February 6 - 2028 January 25 Fire Goat	
2028	2028 January 26 - 2029 February 12 Earth Monkey	
2029	2029 February 13 - 2030 February 2 Earth Rooster	
2030	2030 February 3 - 2031 January 22 Metal Dog	
2031	2031 January 23 - 2032 February 10 Metal Pig	

Your Ascendant according to the Chinese Horoscope.

Along with your Chinese horoscope sign, you also have an ascendant determined by your birth time. This animal will have a strong influence on the image you project to others, and on the events of your life. You should also read the horoscope for the animal that represents your ascendant.

This sign of the ascendant symbolizes the energy that you can develop, and the characteristics that, with effort, you can acquire. That is the reason sometimes we have different attributes from those related to our sign.

In the Chinese horoscope it is amazingly simple to determine your ascendant, the only data you need is your birth time.

Time of birth   **Animal ascendant**

11.00 p.m. to 12.59 a.m. Rat

1.00 a.m. to 2.59 a.m. Ox

3.00 a.m. to 4.59 a.m. Tigre

5.00 a.m. to 6.59 a.m. Rabbit

7.00 a.m. to 8.59 a.m. Dragon

9.00 a.m. to 10.59 a.m. Snake

11:00 a.m. to 12:59 p.m. Horse

1.00 p.m. to 2.59 p.m. Goat

3.00 p.m. to 4.59 p.m. Monkey

5.00 p.m. to 6.59 p.m. Rooster

7.00 p.m. to 8.59 p.m. Dog

9.00 p.m. to 10. 59 p.m. Pig

Combinations of Ascendants and Signs.

Rat Ascendants

Rat ascendant Rat.

They were born from 11 pm to 1 am. They are very friendly people with everyone, although sometimes they are individualistic and materialistic. They are enthusiastic about everything that interests them.

Rat ascendant Ox.

They were born from 1 am to 3 am. They are very reserved and sensible individuals. They project an image of vulnerability, but are strong internally, and have a lot of discipline.

Tiger rising Rat.

They were born from 3 am to 5 am. They are strict, and it is difficult to live with them. They are capricious and tenacious. They like adventures and have new projects in mind constantly.

Rabbit rising Rat.

They were born from 5 am to 7 am. They are successful because of their mischievousness and talent. They have good business luck and good intuition.

Dragon Rising Rat

They were born from 7 am to 9 am. They are leaders par excellence. They thrive in everything they set out to do. They have infinite energy.

Snake rising Rat.

They were born from 9 am to 11 am. They are intuitive and cautious. However, they know how to avoid dangers. They always come out on top.

Rat rising Horse.

They were born from 11 am to 1 pm. They are enthusiastic and impulsive. But they know how to get their way in all situations.

Rat ascendant Goat

They were born from 1 pm to 3 pm. They are cordial and friendly individuals. They love parties. They are positive, but they are codependent.

Rat ascendant Monkey

They were born from 3 pm to 5 pm. They are entrepreneurial for business. They are always thinking about the next step they must take.

Rooster rising Rat.

They were born from 5 pm to 7 pm. They are good salespeople and have a very agile mind. Although they earn a lot of money, they do not know how to manage it, but they soon run out of it.

Dog rising Rat.

They were born from 7 pm to 9 pm. They are mediators and philanthropists. In business they are honest. People esteem them for their loyalty.

Rat ascending Pig

They were born from 9 pm to 11 pm. They are self-reliant, a bit of a hermit and do not mind working for themselves. They are peaceful.

Ox Ascendants

Ox rising Rat.

They were born from 11 pm to 1 am. They are stubborn, but the strength of the Rat sign pushes them to be more approachable and expressive.

Ox ascending Ox.

Born from 1 am to 3 am. Demanding, competitive, inflexible, meticulous, orderly people. They always want to be in charge and believe they are the best. They do not want anyone to tell them what to do and do not take orders from anyone.

Ox rising Tiger.

They were born from 3 am to 5 am. The influence of the Tiger gives him a nature opposite to his sign. He is impulsive, and harsh. Sometimes he has an explosive temperament.

Ox rising Rabbit.

They were born from 5 am to 7 am. He is very natural, serene, and not very affable. He enjoys being at home. He is very loyal.

Ox rising Dragon.

They were born from 7 am to 9 am. They are ambitious with money. They crave power. They are impatient and enterprising.

Snake ascending Ox

Born from 9 am to 11 am. Selfish and autonomous. They are not interested in interacting with others.

Ox rising Horse.

Born from 11 am to 1 pm. The sociable nature of the Horse causes this Ox to be more risk-taking and to project opposite behaviors than it normally would.

Ox ascending Goat.

Born from 1 pm to 3 pm. They use their charisma to obtain their purposes. They are manipulative.

Monkey ascendant Ox

They were born from 3 pm to 5 pm. They focus more on their personal life than their professional life. They are empathetic.

Ox ascending Rooster.

Born from 5 pm to 7 pm. He is arrogant, has a lot of self-confidence, and no one can contradict him. He is critical of others, but not self-critical.

Ox ascending Dog.

They were born from 7 pm to 9 pm. The energies of the Dog will give them a degree of melancholy that will paralyze them. This combination tends to pessimism.

Ox ascending Pig.

Born from 9 pm to 11 pm. Pig energies will motivate you to be affectionate and loving. They are very generous.

Tiger Ascendants

Tiger rising Rat.

They were born from 11pm to 1 am. Super intelligent to negotiate. Their instincts are sharp. Enthusiastic in love and independent. They have a very sympathetic personality.

Tiger ascendant Ox

They were born from 1 am to 3 am. Excellent combination, since the Ox offers harmony to the Tiger, therefore, they will be reflective and less violent.

Tiger rising Tiger.

They were born from 3am to 5am. They are irritable and enthusiastic. Their actions are unpredictable, for that reason they tend to make mistakes.

Tiger rising Rabbit.

They were born from 5 am to 7 am. The energies of the Rabbit make them prudent and methodical; this is a safeguard to not be involved in conflicts.

Tiger rising Dragon.

They were born from 7 am to 9 am. They are ambitious, with sky-high self-esteem. They are courageous and empathetic.

Tiger rising Snake.

They were born from 9 am to 11 am. This combination is not extremely healthy as they tend to be irritable people. On the positive side, they are particularly good at speculative business.

Tiger rising Horse.

They were born from 11 am to 1 pm. They are kind, generous, and giving people. They are always in love with love.

Tiger rising Goat.

They were born from 1 pm to 3 pm. The Goat placates the reckless nature of the Tiger, this is beneficial as it allows him to plan.

Tiger rising Monkey.

They were born from 3 pm to 5 pm. They are friendly and have an incomparable sense of humor. They are insightful, and practical.

Tiger ascendant Rooster

They were born from 5 pm to 7 pm. They are sometimes egocentric. They are meticulous, but highly intelligent.

Tiger rising Dog.

They were born from 7 pm to 9 pm. They are Rational and calm. When they want something, they are relentless.

Tiger rising Pig.

They were born from 9 pm to 11 pm. These Tigers are calm and homely. They prefer to share with their family members Rather than with other people.

Rabbit Ascendants

Rabbit rising Rat.

They were born from 11pm to 1 am. They are mischievous. Rat energies influence this Rabbit to be more affable and cordial.

Rabbit ascendant Ox

They were born from 1 am to 3 am. They are diligent and determined. They always achieve their goals because they are very self-confident.

Rabbit rising Tiger.

They were born from 3 am to 5 am. Sometimes they are aggressive and have surprising changes of temperament. The good thing is that they could control themselves and keep their balance.

Rabbit rising Rabbit.

They were born from 5 am to 7 am. They are discreet, they hate to be the center of attention. They hate unexpected changes. They are remarkably familiar.

Dragon Rising Rabbit

They were born from 7 am to 9 am. They are proud and like to keep their distance from others. They are calculating.

Rabbit rising Snake.

They were born from 9 am to 11 am. They like to live isolated from society. Although they are apathetic, they always have clever ideas and accomplish their goals.

Rabbit rising Horse.

They were born from 11 am to 1 pm. They have a lot of self-confidence and courage to accomplish what they set out to do, and they always achieve their goals in a brief period.

Rabbit rising Goat.

They were born from 1 pm to 3 pm. They are creative and fanciful. Sometimes they live on false ideas.

Rabbit rising Monkey.

They were born from 3 pm to 5 pm. They are nice and have an optimism that contaminates. Sometimes they cross the border with their jokes and offend others.

Rabbit ascendant Rooster

They were born from 5 pm to 7 pm. They are extroverted and communicative. They have a great facility to make friends.

Rabbit rising Dog.

They were born from 7 pm to 9 pm. They are confident and love to share with their friends. They are generous.

Rabbit rising Pig.

They were born from 9 pm to 11 pm. They are very understanding, and kind, the perfect shoulder to cry on. Sometimes they are perfectionists.

Dragon Ascendants

Dragon rising Rat.

They were born from 11pm to 1 am. They are apathetic, but business savvy. They are diplomatic when they want to get something.

Dragon ascendant Ox

They were born from 1 am to 3 am. They are not friendly. They are hermits, and manipulative. They achieve their purposes because they are persevering.

Dragon rising Tiger.

They were born from 3 am to 5 am. Particularly good lovers, meticulous. They are impulsive at times as they get carried away by their emotions.

Dragon rising Rabbit.

They were born from 5 am to 7 am. They are balanced in all senses. They can become apathetic and nervous.

Dragon Ascending Dragon

They were born from 7 am to 9 am. They are manipulative, they do not like anyone to contradict them. They are stubborn, but good leaders.

Snake rising Dragon.

They were born from 9 am to 11 am. They are overly ambitious and intelligent. They like to impose their will when it comes to achieving their goals.

Dragon rising Horse.

Born from 11 am to 1 pm. Seducers par excellence, and chatterboxes. They like parties and events of many people.

Dragon ascendant Goat

They were born from 1 pm to 3 pm. They are slow and prudent. They always act politely and have many friends.

Monkey rising Dragon.

They were born from 3 pm to 5 pm. They have charisma and the power to dominate others with their smile. Their intelligence combined with their charms causes destruction on a social level.

Dragon ascending Rooster

They were born from 5 pm to 7 pm. They are creative, and risk-takers. They are fun, and everyone invites them to their parties because they are cheerful.

Dragon rising Dog.

They were born from 7 pm to 9 pm. They are very tolerant and loyal. Their kindness is incomparable. They are always ready to help. They have a vocation for service.

Dragon rising Pig.

They were born from 9 pm to 11 pm. They are very balanced, and calm. They prefer to spend extended periods of solitude to think and calculate their steps.

Ascendants of the Snake

Snake ascending Rat

They were born from 11pm to 1 am. They are affectionate, traditional, and familiar. They am kind.

Ascending Snake Ox

They were born from 1 am to 3 am. They are extraordinarily strong in character. They are intelligent and insightful.

Tiger rising Snake.

They were born from 3 am to 5 am. They are very distrustful and brusque. Sometimes they are aggressive.

Rabbit rising Snake.

They were born from 5 am to 7 am. They are calculating and manipulative. They are very solitary and shy.

Dragon Ascending Snake

They were born from 7 am to 9 am. They are successful and like to constantly make changes in their lives without counting on others. Very self-confident.

Snake ascending Snake

They were born from 9 am to 11 am. They are hermits and distrustful. Their ideas are always accurate. They have a lot of enthusiasm.

Snake ascending Horse

They were born from 11 am to 1 pm. They are very cheerful but calculating. They are seductive and always get what they want.

Snake ascending Goat

They were born from 1 pm to 3 pm. They are naive, creative, and very enterprising. They always must be doing something; they are very hyperactive.

Snake ascending Monkey

They were born from 3 pm to 5 pm. They are super fun and cheerful. Their friendliness is contagious. They are easy to make friends with.

Rooster rising Snake.

They were born from 5 pm to 7 pm. They are authoritarian, egocentric, and competitive. They are stubborn and stubborn.

Snake ascending Dog

They were born from 7 pm to 9 pm. They are empathetic, kind, and cunning. Sometimes they like to win at the expense of others.

Snake ascending Pig

They were born from 9 pm to 11 pm. They are charming and helpful. Their ego goes to infinity, and this brings them into conflict with others.

Ascendants of the Horse

Horse ascendant Rat

They were born from 11pm to 1 am. They are friendly, cheerful, and good friends. They are seductive and good analytical people.

Rising Horse Ox

They were born from 1 am to 3 am. They are profoundly serious. They are extremely easy to concentrate, and what they set out to do, they accomplish.

Rising Horse Tiger

They were born from 3 am to 5 am. They are brave and very sure of what they want. They have a fantastic and enviable vision of the future.

Rising Horse Rabbit

They were born from 5 am to 7 am. They are romantic, affectionate, and enthusiastic. They are diligent and supportive.

Dragon Rising Horse

They were born from 7 am to 9 am. They have great self-esteem. Sometimes they are anxious and see ghosts where there are none.

Snake ascending Horse

They were born from 9 am to 11 am. They are not sociable, but they are family oriented. They are highly intelligent and lucky in love.

Horse rising Horse.

They were born from 11 am to 1 pm. They are successful and fun. Sometimes they are nervous and self-centered when they lose a battle.

Horse ascending Goat

They were born from 1 pm to 3 pm. They are calm and serene. They have a great power of concentration.

Monkey rising Horse.

They were born from 3 pm to 5 pm. They are achievers and highly intelligent. Everything they set their minds to they achieve. They are lucky in love.

Horse ascending Rooster

They were born from 5 pm to 7 pm. They are brave and obstacles do not paralyze them, they are very self-confident, live calm and happy.

Horse ascending Dog

They were born from 7 pm to 9 pm. They are traditional, familiar, and loyal. They are honest and sincere.

Horse ascending Pig

They were born from 9 pm to 11 pm. They are social and fanciful. Sometimes they are a little lazy. They are lucky in games of chance.

Goat Ascendants

Rat ascendant Goat

They were born from 11pm to 1 am. They are very mischievous and like to take advantage of others. They have an incredible power of seduction that allows them to get where they want to go.

Goat ascendant Ox

They were born from 1 am to 3 am. They are very responsible and planful. They are creative and always have ideas that allow them to accomplish their goals.

Ascending Tiger Goat

They were born from 3 am to 5 am. They are very exaggerated when it comes to communicating. They are successful in their lives and are lucky in love.

Rabbit ascendant Goat

They were born from 5 am to 7 am. They are lazy, they follow the law of the least effort. They do not like to commit themselves sentimentally. Everything that requires commitment they repel it.

Dragon Ascending Goat

They were born from 7 am to 9 am. They have an otherworldly courage and strength. They are the people who get involved in projects that other signs do not do for fear of failure.

Snake ascendant Goat

They were born from 9 am to 11 am. They are cautious but brave. They plan everything. They never go beyond their limits.

Horse ascendant Goat

They were born from 11 am to 1 pm. They are skillful, dreamers and enthusiastic. They are incredibly lucky in love, but unlucky for money.

Ascending Goat

They were born from 1 pm to 3 pm. They are a catastrophe, doubtful and insecure. They are slow to act because they think too much. They are sometimes treacherous.

Monkey ascendant Goat

They were born from 3 pm to 5 pm. They are fun, enthusiastic, and kind. They are the soul of the night, and they have a lot of talent to conquer.

Rooster ascendant Goat

They were born from 5 pm to 7 pm. They are intelligent and shrewd. Sometimes they are insecure and need to consult with others before acting.

Goat ascending Dog.

They were born from 7 pm to 9 pm. They are polite and balanced, but very codependent on the people they love. They need constant protection.

Goat ascending Pig.

They were born from 9 pm to 11 pm. They are very suspicious, inclined to sadness. They are very stubborn.

Monkey Ascendant

Rat rising Monkey.

They were born from 11pm to 1 am. They are overly cautious. They have an incredible ability to achieve their goals, even if they encounter the biggest obstacle along the way.

Ox Rising Monkey

They were born from 1 am to 3 am. They are complicated, full of internal contradictions. They do not have agility of thought, and this leads them to fail at times.

Tiger Rising Monkey

They were born from 3 am to 5 am. They are very enthusiastic, but their egocentrism makes them fail. They possess an inexhaustible source of energy.

Rabbit rising Monkey.

They were born from 5 am to 7 am. They are prudent, but also intelligent. They are discreet and choose their friends very well.

Dragon Rising Monkey

They were born from 7 am to 9 am. They are greedy, and brave. They are not enthusiastic. They like to focus on what they want and do not stop until they get it.

Snake rising Monkey.

They were born from 9 am to 11 am. Their power of seduction is enhanced by their intelligence. They always succeed because they calculate the pros and cons of a situation.

Rising Horse Monkey

They were born from 11 am to 1 pm. They are lazy and have little power of concentration. They act, but sometimes it is late and so they miss opportunities.

Monkey ascendant Goat

They were born from 1 pm to 3 pm. They have a very keen sixth sense. They are romantic and creative.

Mono ascending Monkey

They were born from 3 pm to 5 pm. They are anxious and interested. They have a volatile temperament.

Rising Monkey Rooster

They were born from 5 pm to 7 pm. They love risks. They are optimistic and successful in everything they undertake.

Upward Dog Monkey

They were born from 7 pm to 9 pm. They are generous and loyal. They do not accept lies, even if they are pious.

Monkey ascendant Pig

They were born from 9 pm to 11 pm. They are balanced and calm. They are not very sociable; they prefer to be alone.

Rooster Ascendant

Rooster rising Rat.

They were born from 11pm to 1 am. They are aggressive and brave. They are egocentric and narcissistic.

Rooster ascendant Ox

They were born from 1 am to 3 am. They are honest and outgoing. They tell the truth, even if it hurts, to anyone. They are traditional and familiar.

Rooster rising Tiger.

They were born from 3 am to 5 am. They are very conflictive. Sometimes they do things without thinking and that leads them to fail. They are hasty.

Rooster rising Rabbit.

They were born from 5 am to 7 am. They are quiet, they like to keep a low profile in all situations. They are diligent workers.

Dragon Rising Rooster

They were born from 7 am to 9 am. They are selfish and dominant. They like to take revenge on those they feel have wronged them.

Rooster rising Snake.

They were born from 9 am to 11 am. They are analytical and reflective. They always think twice before taking a step to avoid making a mistake.

Rooster rising Horse.

They were born from 11 am to 1 pm. They are particularly good friends, but if someone betrays them, they are very spiteful. They like to work, but they also like to have fun.

Rooster ascending Goat

They were born from 1 pm to 3 pm. They are sensible and thoughtful. They never meddle in the lives of others and choose their friends very cautiously.

Rooster rising Monkey.

They were born from 03 pm to 5 pm. They are very diligent and responsible. Their energy is extremely high, and they have the power to concentrate and achieve their purposes, even if there are obstacles in their way.

Rooster ascending Rooster

They were born from 5 pm to 7 pm. They are authoritarian. Their pride is incomparable. When they want something, they do not stop until they get it, and they get anyone out of the way.

Rooster ascending Dog

They were born from 7 pm to 9 pm. They are very tolerant and empathetic. They are very family oriented and loving.

Rooster ascending Pig

They were born from 9 pm to 11 pm. They are very discreet and kind. They always like to help whoever needs it, without asking for anything in return.

Ascendants of the Dog

Rat rising Dog.

Born from 11pm to 01 am. Enthusiastic to the bone. Courageous and hardworking. Loyal and tolerant.

Ox rising Dog.

They were born from 1 am to 3 am. They are kind, but solitary. They help, but do not like ties. If someone contradicts them, they become authoritarian.

Tiger rising Dog.

They were born from 3 am to 5 am. They are brave and daring. When they love you to death, but when they hate you, they are capable of disappearing.

Rabbit rising Dog.

They were born from 5 am to 7 am. They are cowardly, shy, and introverted. They tend to be pessimistic for no reason. They avoid conflicts and miss opportunities.

Dragon rising Dog.

They were born from 7 am to 9 am. They are vain and talkative. They can become selfish. They like to help, and others can take advantage of them.

Snake rising Dog.

They were born from 9 am to 11 am. They are vain, not spontaneous. Their distant nature causes them to have few friends. They are persevering.

Horse rising Dog.

They were born from 11 am to 1 pm. They are kind and loyal. They tend to depression.

Ascending Goat

They were born from 1 pm to 3 pm. They always pay a lot of attention to their chores. They have a strong character and get angry easily.

Monkey rising Dog.

Born from 3 pm to 5 pm. They are hardworking and formal to fulfill their commitments. They love to give what they have.

Rooster rising Dog.

They were born from 5 pm to 7 pm. They are ambitious. They avoid confrontations and prefer to follow orders from others to avoid conflicts.

Dog rising Dog.

They were born from 7 pm to 9 pm. They are very suspicious. They do not tolerate or accept advice from others. They are very judicious and always make the best decisions at the right time.

Pig rising Dog.

They were born from 9 pm to 11 pm. They are particularly good analytical people. They have a capacity for abstraction and can invent new things.

Pig Ascendants

Tiger rising Pig.

They were born from 3 am to 5 am. They have a warrior nature. They are ambitious. They always succeed because they are persevering.

Pig rising Rabbit.

They were born from 5 am to 7 am. Super enthusiastic. Sociable nature. Uses their friendships to achieve their goals.

Dragon rising Pig.

They were born from 7 am to 9 am. They are impulsive. One of the best lovers. It is meticulous and romantic. They are lucky in games of chance.

Snake Ascending Pig

They were born from 9 am to 11 am. They are persevering and like to plan. They are sometimes calculating.

Pig rising Horse.

They were born from 11 am to 1 pm. They are egocentric. They possess the quality of taking from themselves to favor others. They can focus on their goals despite obstacles.

Pig rising Goat.

They were born from 1 pm to 3 pm. They are supportive and balanced. Sometimes they tend to be annoyed by the successes of others.

Monkey rising Pig.

They were born from 3 pm to 5 pm. They are intelligent and ambitious. Sometimes they have opinions about things they do not know. They do not know how to control their impulses.

Rooster ascendant Pig

They were born from 5 pm to 7 pm. They live most of the time in a fantasy world. They make many mistakes in their life because they do not pay attention to details.

Pig rising Dog.

They were born from 7 pm to 9 pm. They are affable so they have many friends. They are disciplined and organized.

Pig rising Pig.

They were born from 9 pm to 11 pm. They are happy, luck always smiles on them. They achieve their goals with ease. They are mature and responsible.

Chinese Element of the Year 2024, Wood

The element of the year 2024 is wood. Wood is a creative element. If this element corresponds to you because of your year of birth, you should channel these energies creatively. Wood symbolizes compassion and tolerance. If you want to take advantage of these energies it is important that you surround yourself with natural plants, flowers, and green objects throughout the year.

Wood is an element related to the ability to project and make decisions, therefore, the year 2024 will be a year of development, evolution, and flourishing.

This element is related to digestion, respiration, heart, and metabolism, and in traditional Chinese medicine, it guarantees a continuous energetic flow. In relation to feelings this translates into the correct expression of our emotions.

Wood will help us gain awareness and understanding of objective reality during 2024. It will bring us firmness and empathy in our relationships. Wood, being related to our personality, will bring us the right dose of enthusiasm, decisiveness, and dynamism to act and face all the challenges of this year.

Wood is the element we need this year to be able to make the necessary decisions, for changes that are essential. Thanks to this element we will have the right strategies and the ability to organize and maintain control over all processes, but we will also maintain flexibility.

Who is the Wooden Dragon?

The Wood Dragon is a highly creative individual who enjoys trying their luck in all areas of their life. They are famous for displaying original ideas and being focused. Dragons have a flamboyant personality, exude sensuality, are lustful and have a strong attraction to a different sex.

In China it is believed that the year of the Dragon is the most prosperous and blessed, and traditionally it is the most esteemed animal. There are legends that relate that the emperors are the reincarnation in this life of the Dragons. The Wood Dragon is cheerful and loves to party and have fun, sometimes they only think about having fun and have no desire to take life seriously.

The Dragon with its magical powers can soar to ethereal heights or dive into the depths of the ocean. The Dragon is skilled, strong, and powerful, yet possesses a magnetic aura, is intuitive, and prosperous. Dragons are best suited to be leaders because of their attributes, character, and passion.

Armed with natural courage, tenacity and intelligence, Dragons are enthusiastic and naive. They are never afraid of challenges and accept any compromise. However, Dragons are sometimes violent, and they do not hate criticism.

Dragons love to be outdoors, so during the year 2024 there will be transformations related to energy preservation, technology, care of the sea and climate change issues. Technology will see extraordinary progress that will be applied to the environmental area, social networks, and digital business.

Dragons have an overview of everything that is happening, so this is a year to produce something in community and spread change globally.

During the Wood Dragon years everything seems more gigantic, and this applies to misfortunes as well as triumphs, so we are likely to experience extreme weather and natural catastrophes. However, with the nobility, kindness and mercy of the Wood Dragon, all people will come together to encourage and support each other, increasing our sense of empathy.

Being pious and charitable is most important this year 2024, as well as sharing time with your family and close friends. As we become more united, communication will be our most valuable tool to maintain peace globally, as well as in our lives.

General Predictions for the Year of the Dragon

February 10, 2024, begins the sensational Year of the Green Wood Dragon, and according to Chinese astrology, green symbolizes life, change and growth. The associated planet is Jupiter, a planet that is beneficial; we will reap the fruits sown in 2023.

The Year of the Dragon in 2024 will bring us luck, prosperity, well-being, and progress. We will have many opportunities for growth and transformation, but also challenges and complications, accentuating the need for forgiveness, empathy, and peaceful decisions.

During the years that the element is wood, life rewards people who are sociable and professional. Obtaining a degree, or traveling are some of the possibilities this year.

We will have the opportunity to develop our leadership skills, this is a year for new beginnings and for creating structures that will last for the long term. This year of the Dragon is favorable for change and growth as the energy of the wooden Dragon possesses the ability to inspire innovative ideas and exalt our imagination.

We will live through some stages that will be full of difficulties, but those are the moments when we must use the Dragon's energy to succeed and overcome the challenges. During the year do not forget that the Dragon personifies change and adaptability, characteristics that will help us to grow and renew ourselves.

The year 2024 will be a busy year with possibilities to evolve, we will experience many political, economic, relational, and environmental conflicts, highlighting that peaceful solutions are the answer to any problem.

This year will stimulate us to do new business and develop in the entrepreneurial world because the energy of the Dragon, and its qualities of being courageous and ambitious, will inspire us. We will develop many adaptive capacities, and patience and perseverance will allow us to overcome all adversities and move towards triumph. This is also a propitious year to work on our spiritual growth, it is especially important to keep focused on our goals.

In summary, it will be a year of positive changes and significant advances in our lives where we will have the opportunity to find love, strengthen a relationship, and have economic and spiritual prosperity.

Meaning of the Elements in the Chinese Horoscope

Metal

People born in the years ending in 0 or 1 in the Chinese horoscope are categorized within the metal element. Metal, the material from which shields and swords are made, is the element that symbolizes firmness and honesty, but also severity.

Metal is the element of autumn, the season of harvest and abundance. It is dual as the functions of its element, since in the form of a sword it liquidates, and as a spoon it nourishes. Metal comes from the earth, is dominated by Fire, and transfigures wood.

The personality of these individuals belonging to the metal element tends to be strongly ambivalent. They do best when they are alone, as they are not accountable to anyone.

They are determined, forgers of their destiny, stubborn, professional, and indifferent to any attempt at compromise. Their freedom is paramount, and it is useless to try to pressure them, let alone help them, because they do not listen to anyone and do not accept intrusions and impediments. They choose to rely only on themselves, and do not allow themselves to be impressed by anyone, since they are powerful and capable of performing great works.

For them there are no difficulties that can stop them, and even if a situation becomes untenable, they resist to the end. They are ambitious and calculating, they love money, power, and success, and will spare no means to achieve their goals, even if it means breaking relationships.

They are designed for careers that empower them to express their element: jewelers, financiers, insurance of any kind, locksmiths, miners, surgeons, and for any context that allows them to distinguish themselves from others. They can also be successful in professions connected with wood or paper. Those related to water will be beneficial, those related to earth may cause them conflicts and they should stay away from those related to the fire element.

They are not interested in feelings, and are not moved by the difficulties of others, to the point of manipulating them if they can gain an advantage. Those who suffer the consequences are specifically the people of the wood element since it manipulates and subdues them with frontal aggressions. However, people of the water element, as they are receptive, receive an effective push that benefits them enormously. The only ones who can really bend them are individuals belonging to the Fire element, as they dominate their insensitivity and severity with a contagious emotion.

Physically you can recognize a person of the metal element by their sad look and the anemic color of their face. They are fragile, prone to stress, and can be affected by temperature changes and poor nutrition. That is why they should stimulate their appetite, emphasizing spicy foods.

The most favorable season for them is autumn, and during this time they can develop their potentialities to the maximum, although this does not mean that they should overdo it or be stubborn. He should wear white clothes, use metals, and white quartz as amulets.

Metal is rigid and rigid, not afraid of danger. It is an independent type of person, who, driven by greed, proceeds with perseverance, concentrates on success, plans, and detests the spontaneous. Once he adopts a path, he does not change it. Despite their external insensitivity, people of this element radiate a magnetism that is perceived by all with whom they connect. However, to benefit from their abilities, they must learn to be less Dogmatic as this interferes with their relationships.

People born under the metal element must educate themselves, so that they can express their emotions. If they do not do so, they will feel that their energies are diminished.

Earth

People born in the years ending in the numbers 8 or 9 belong to the earth element. To this element correspond the characteristics of steadfastness, persistence, and fecundity. Although in Chinese astrology, Earth does not have a season of its own, it is related in the calendar to the last two or three weeks of the other seasons.

Earth is the element that represents stability and tangibility, but if there is an excess it transforms people into cautious, suspicious, and stubborn, restricting their initiatives and fantasies.

The person of the earth element is patient and humble, always works with constancy, without giving himself an instant of rejoicing or disorder. He never tires and can be as eager and materialistic as he is naive and prudent. His most unquestionable characteristic is his accentuated discouragement. He is too serious, loves to plan and direct, is horrified by coincidences, and, although he is intelligent and has an exceptional memory, it bothers him to appear resplendent.

Insatiably reflective, ambitious, and anxious, it is thus exposed to recharge the spleen, an organ related to this element, and which is weakened when the person has a sharp mentality.

The person who belongs to this element cements personal relationships gradually but endures for a long time. It is very devoted and defender in love, always ready to contract and fulfill their responsibilities, and although it is not demonstrative in their emotions is a shoulder that can always be counted on because it will be at your side in the moments you need it.

In their work they are serious and retiring, but also organized and dependable. They are the right people to conduct business with morality, austerity, and fireproof honesty. Their reasoning makes them unbeatable intermediaries in the problems, contributing with their own practical and opportune exits. They are competent for professions that require dexterity, but do not involve taking initiatives, or leadership situations. Although she is not an easy person to bear, because of her capriciousness and nostalgia, and her inability to be cheerful, she connects well with the metal element, to which she instills stability, and with water, which she manages to contain and govern skillfully.

It usually has conflicts with the wood element, since, although it protects it at times it also suffocates it, and with Fire, which drives it as much as it weakens it.
The earth element is related to the planet Saturn. You must be incredibly careful with the consumption of sweets, something that you love since it is related to your element. They should always choose the natural sweet and limit the use of white sugar as this destroys the calcium in their bone system. His other weak point is the digestive system, which usually punishes him strongly, for that reason he should keep a light and easily digestible diet. It is recommended that they seek direct contact with Mother Earth, walking barefoot in the sand or in the field.

Its lucky color is yellow, and its quartz is topaz and citrine.

Earth represents wealth, reasonableness, materialism, and security. These people tend to be introspective which makes them have a great capacity for reasoning. The Earth is the container of life and this seals of indelible form to those born under the influence of this element, since they are stable people in whom you can delegate. The earth feeds on fire, generating great energy that heats and melts metal, can subdue water, and can be consumed by wood. To feel good, the person of the earth element needs material security, although it should be noted that they are industrious, formal, and organized. They can be reproached for being pretentious, but because of their merits they advance towards their goals slowly, obtaining stable results.

Fire

People born in the years ending in 6 or 7 correspond to the fire element. To this element belong passion, courage, and leadership. The fire element is the element of the summer season, where everything fructifies and reaches its consummation. It is related to the planet Mars, beneficial, but sometimes impulsive. It is excessively sterile and symbolizes the person who excels, but also mistreats others. Combative, vain, and irritable, the person of this element goes from anger to unbridled joy.

Since childhood he has had a leadership personality, ambition is present in his life, he likes dangers, laughter, enthusiasm, and conflict. Difficulties, instead of discouraging him, incite him to proceed, and in these cases, he undergoes a violent metamorphosis.

These people were born to win, but they do not know how to admit it, because they do not manage to observe themselves and exploit their energies. They are great in the military area, in sports, and as bosses since the others perish before their charisma. They know how to use the energies of the wood element, using their genius at their service, and induce in people of the earth element the vital courage to move forward.
People of the water element tend to extinguish their passion, and those of the metal element put them to the test with a rigidity that drains their energy field.

The most easily damaged organ in these people is the heart, there is the possibility of tachycardia. In addition, they may suffer from ear and intestinal problems. They should wear clothes of bright colors, among which red prevails, and use as amulets quartz such as garnets and hematite. They should also use incense and candles.

These charismatic, enthusiastic, and opportunistic people communicate well and focus on action. Their selfishness and desire to succeed are incalculable and they rely only on their own views. They tend to neglect details as they are sometimes stubborn and embark on goals that require intense work.

People born under the influence of the fire element are positive, always give their best and get involved in everything they do with love and will. Their energies serve to sustain those around them who lack it.

Fire heats the home; it allows us to prepare food. This element nourishes the earth through the ashes, it feeds on dry wood, which is to say, wood, its heat dominates the metal, which is to say, it makes it flexible, and it can only be dominated by water.

A leader always has an abundance of the fire element and is always inclined to make quick decisions. He is attracted to unconventional ideas, is not afraid of danger, and is always on the move. It is important for him to learn emotional intelligence because arrogance can strengthen his egotism and make him uncontrollable, specifically when he encounters obstacles. This self-destructive style is prominent in youth.

Success accompanies people of the fire element, but they must be overly cautious with instability and restlessness, which are the most usual inadequacies of those born under fire. It is better to master these defects, so as not to be enslaved by them. They should look for a quiet place where they can be at peace, and meditation will also bring them balance.

People of the fire element are tenacious and lucrative.

Wood

People born in the years ending in the numbers 4 or 5 belong to the wood element. Wood is the element that symbolizes harmony, beauty, and creativity. They have an extremely high degree of self-confidence, and an iron will, which makes them the right people to fight for a just cause.

Wood is related to the planet Jupiter, it is the most beneficial of the elements, symbol of permanence and knowledge. Adaptable, it bends comfortably, and has multiple uses, characterizing communicative, giving, and honest people.

People of the wood element are creative and vital, but sometimes they are scattered and unable to find their way and fulfill their purposes. They trust others to the point of innocence, and like to rub shoulders with everyone, always discovering new things to divulge and satisfy themselves. They are attracted to nature and children and give priority to family.
Occasionally they tend to have impossible expectations, and have a habit of belittling their bodies, overindulge in food and get caught up in passion and sensuality.
They are accustomed to choosing partners of the water element, from whom they absorb boldness and support, and those of fire, whom they benefit by supplying with their brilliant ideas.
It does not get along very well with the metal element, which ruins it mercilessly.

The Wood element is recognized by its greenish color. These people should take care of their eyes.

Wood is used to build shelters, which is why it protects us. Wood coincides with the creativity of water, and thanks to this quality they understand and help others.

Those born under the wood element have internal conflicts to submit to rules and traditions where severe judgment is constantly in force. This element nourishes water and, at the same time, is fuel for fire. Its energy is sucked by earth and subjugated by metal.

People of the wood element always obtain great triumphs and have a coveted structure. Their vocations are versatile. They attach immense importance to integrity, striving to find a permanent place in life. Belief in success, and their analytical skills give them the ability to tackle the most complex problems without hesitation. With an incredible power of conviction, they function in many areas, as they always aim for development and transformation.

Their natural will helps them to move forward, and they always find support and the necessary capital, since other people count on their ability to transform ideas into wealth.

Its main obstacle is to take things to the extreme. Anger, and restrained anger negatively affect the energies of this element. Being near trees and touching them balances the wood element.

At work, individuals belonging to the wood element are orderly, intelligent, and resourceful. In commercial activities, they are more fruitful when the work is teamwork, and is well structured.

No area of work related to their element is unfavorable, but those related to fire may affect them, and those related to metal will ruin them.

Water

The most insensitive and tenebrous element, affine to winter, longevity, and the planet Mercury, is the ruler of communication and deep affections.

An individual of the water element is sensitive, but hermetic. He is charitable, sentimental, and fragile, hates criticism and, for this reason, chooses to act covertly to protect himself. He is cordial, eloquent and at the same time prudent, and knows how to overcome setbacks without showing off, with cunning, shrewdness and perseverance. In this way he achieves his goals, indirectly and silently, giving the impression of being considerate and understanding. Lack of energy is a problem for the water element if it does not learn to balance its powerlessness with the strength that comes from reflection and communication with the deepest parts of its being. Panic is always the guiding cord of his dramatic life, often lived in darkness for fear of showing himself and fighting.

On the professional level, they are inhibited by competition, however, they perform well in clear and sheltered places, such as schools, bookstores, editorial offices or any place where communication, oral or written, is the primary mechanism, and in the company of peaceful colleagues who fit their personality, such as, for example, someone of the wood element, with whom coincides the desire for wisdom, or with the metal, from whom they obtain decision. Conversely, he does not adapt to the fire element, whom he extinguishes and discourages, nor to individuals belonging to the earth element, with whom he feels limited, conditioned, and hindered.

The black color is the one that favors them, but they should use it with moderation because it tends to discourage them. The same happens with dark quartz, which attract luck, such as jet, onyx, and tourmaline. To make the best use of its qualities, without going to extremes, and to avoid dispersion, the person of the water element should begin his plans in the winter.

In positive periods, the love relationships of this element transmit tenderness, equanimity and caution, potentials that enable them to conduct themselves with the necessary sagacity to remedy the origin of their conflicts when they appear. They have an incredible capacity for reasoning, although their reserved, deep, and turbid personality leads them to be prone to melancholy. They also lack confidence and boldness. Creativity is one of the main characteristics that represent this element, as well as adaptation, gentleness, mercy, and sympathy. Without water there would be no living beings on earth, this element is pure and crystalline, qualities that have those who belong to this element.

People belonging to this element are affable and have a wonderful command over others. They have an original intuition, which allows them to conquer quickly. Endurance, and lucidity gives them the opportunity to predict events.

They can perceive the faculties of others, inspire them effectively, but they are discreet and will not let others notice that they are using them.

Abuses with sodium or alkaloids, and life prototypes that deviate from common structures are very harmful for people born under the water element. Respecting the hours of sleep, maintaining a relaxed mental and emotional health, and having contact with water restores their harmony, and optimizes their energies.

Those who belong to a water element sign can have professions related to wood and fire and be successful, have jobs that relate to their own element, and decline careers, functions and jobs that relate to earth, as earth subdues water.

Compatibility and Incompatibility

They are compatible:

Rat - Dragon - Monkey.

They relate to each other through their personalities which are continually active and friendly. All three are diligent, impatient, enthusiastic, and restless, and always have high aspirations in mind. They are full of ideas, have the stamina and courage required to execute them, always producing innovative, unexpected, surprising, and powerful solutions.

Tiger - Horse - Dog.

They are connected by the satisfaction they feel when they interact. They are united by their modesty, dignity, honesty, and stubborn altruism. Insightful, astute, and communicative, although a bit violent and strict, they fight vigorously against inequalities, violence, and illegalities. These three signs never sell their conscience.

Ox - Snake - Rooster.

These three signs are united by their formality, reasonableness, and the seriousness they achieve in their lives. Energetic, enterprising, and tireless, inflexible in their resolutions, they like to reconsider and plan calmly before obtaining commitments that they would regret later.

Their lack is coldness, since for them reason must prevail over emotions.

Rabbit -Goat -Pig.

Three emotional signs that are also united by their creativity. Instinctive, susceptible, sensitive, and withdrawn, they easily adapt to their habitat, and as good profiteers they do not mind depending on others. Their daily affirmations always carry implicitly the words: perfection, alliance, and conformity.

Note: Opposite signs are opposite enemies:

Rat - Horse - Ox - Goat Tiger - Monkey

Rabbit - Rooster - Dragon - Dog - Snake - Pig.

Characteristics of the Chinese Zodiac Signs

Rat

Characteristics

Rats are shrewd animals. They know how to overcome difficulties in an intelligent way, even if they get entangled in them continuously. They are shrewd since they manipulate some circumstances to their convenience. They are violent, they try to reach their goals quickly, focusing on getting to the end, even if that means suffering or distressing others.

At work, your colleagues will feel very helpless because they cannot work at your pace, and even if it is not your intention, you will make many enemies. You will try to obtain the most important positions in your company. Nothing will stop you; you will have no scruples because your success is the priority. Money is the important thing in their lives, they will transform everything into money, including their artistic productions, since they have tendencies to creativity. With friends, it is also possible to find disagreements because of this aggressiveness that characterizes them.

In love, Rats have no problem showing their affection, although they are more impulsive than romantic. If the other person does not reciprocate, they will try to get their love by any means.

Despite being thrifty, their power of attraction exerts immense power over others, which is why they will never lack admirers. An individual of the Rat sign looks reserved, but he is not. The person of this sign is very sociable and loves parties. Rats love their friends and family, and often get involved in other people's problems.

The Rat's capacity for love is only surpassed by her mischievousness and attachment to money. She never worries about having someone else to feed and allows her family and friends to stay at her home and find support in her, as the Rat's cautiousness will always make it easy for her to find them an assignment so they can pay the rent.

Rats do not know how to keep secrets well, and when it comes to confidences, they are not very honest, and if they must use the information they have obtained, they can take advantage of other people's mistakes. Although reserved with her feelings, the Rat, when nervous, becomes impertinent and being so dynamic and diligent, she resents laziness and waste. Among its destructive aspects is that it dominates them to confess gossip, to censure, to make analogies, to murmur and to agree.

Rats sometimes buy objects they do not need and are always fooled by discounts. In their mind, and in their home, there will always be an accumulation of memories and affective junk confined. They have a keen eye for trivial things, great retentiveness, and are extraordinarily curious.

They can fight against difficulties and are at ease during conflicts. They act with responsibility and maturity and are shrewd. The obstacle they often encounter is greed. The ambitious Rat will have to have at least one complicated economic downfall in his life for him to understand that stinginess does not pay off,

The Rat is attracted to people of the sign of the Ox, in whom they find strength, confidence, and the devotion they offer.

Powerful Dragons are also compatible with the Rat. They find Snakes intelligent and attractive, with whom they establish beneficial partnerships. Because authority and radiance hypnotize, the Rat will always fall prey to the Monkey's unwavering spell and has a similarity to the skill with which the Monkey acts.

It will always have conflicts with the sign of the Horse, too autonomous for the Rat's singularity. His relationship with the Rooster is also unwise because his idealism exasperates the Rat's materialistic sense. His relationship with the Goat is fatal, since with his happiness he would squander the Rat's savings.

Ox

Characteristics

Oxen are conformable and serene animals. They appreciate work, though not enough to spend all day at it. They savor their leisure time and always find something to enrapture their lives with. They are people who project a courteous personality, and conversations with them are smooth and pleasant. However, they detest controversy, and prefer to be right Rather than to provoke an upset over a conflict. He does not mind being the one who agrees in most scenarios, although there is a possibility that one day he will explode and amaze everyone with misconduct.

He hates getting entangled in conflicts and prefers a comfortable, steady, and stable job, even if it pays poorly, since what he cannot stand is the stress of a better paid one. He never leaves things half done, even if he must use more time to complete them. Although they do not like to argue, they do like to order and be respected, which is why we are likely to see Oxen in positions of authority. They will be a pleasant and comfortable leader to deal with if they are not antagonized.

Outside of working hours, they are affectionate and never mistreat the people they live with. If they are left to do what they plan, and no one pokes their noses into their affairs, coexistence will be excellent.

In love they are jealous people, for that reason it is necessary to be careful not to cloud their peace. They are faithful and demand the same from their partner. They are sensual lovers, and coexistence with the Ox is good, if we understand that everything he initiates is done with good intentions.

People who like to inquire about their partner's past and want to manipulate, do not suit a relationship with the Ox, because he loves peace, and hates to communicate things from his past.

The Ox is aware that when things are done correctly, lasting success is achieved. He does not believe in fate or luck and will obtain his goals through his stubbornness and hard work. He is trustworthy because he delivers what he promises. Other people's opinions are not important to him. He always devotes himself body and soul to whatever he must do, and never leaves anything half done.

They are not a person of details, do not expect poems or songs, because their gifts will always be simple and without presumptions. Being so traditional they have tendencies to long relationships, as they require time to reach a relationship of enough trust. They are phlegmatic to change and let their true emotions show. Never despise an Ox as they are worth their weight in gold, besides their mind has the capacity to keep even the last detail of a humiliation for a long time.

The Ox hates to be in debt, he will always pay what he owes, and for him it is unforgivable not to be grateful. You will never hear from his mouth words of gratitude because he thinks that actions speak louder than words. You must be incredibly careful with the Ox's tolerance, because when he loses his patience, he does not reason, although this is exceedingly rare to happen.

In its negative manifestation the Ox is narrow-minded, has no consideration for others, although everyone respects and admires it for its sincerity, and the firmness of its values.

His affable character makes him an architect of great business, as he will always make sure to take all precautionary measures so that prosperity is not lacking in his family. His life revolves around his home and his work, so he prefers calculated, long-term risks.

As he is an individual of moderate habits, insecurity discourages him. The Rooster is the perfect partner for him. Both are powerful and diligent. Relationships with the Rat, or the Snake, will also be beneficial, as both will be intensely committed to the Ox. He does not do well in the company of the Goat, the Tiger, or the Dog, as they are repelled by his excessive formalism.

Tiger

Characteristics

The Tiger is an animal to be admired. They may be spoiled by those closest to them, but they like to keep their distance. Sometimes others, while admiring them, are also suspicious or even jealous.

A Tiger loves everything that involves movement, they are never calm, they always act with courage looking for the most direct path that will lead them to their goals. They have no regard for form, the only important thing for them is speed.

The Tiger's personality is extremely attractive, they communicate very well, and they can be leaders.

A Tiger usually chooses high-risk professions, rejects quiet office professions, or jobs that demand a lot of time before a result is achieved. They will justify their ideas whenever necessary, what they detest about the world they will shout about, and fight to change it. They cannot stand injustice, nor can they stand those who oppose their ideas.

Their ability to fight makes them tireless, and this virtue in love is wonderful. The only problem is that as they love you, they can stop loving you because they are a bit capricious, and as they like risks and adventures, they are predisposed to adultery.

They are not vindictive, they are jealous, spontaneous, affectionate, splendid and possess a unique sense of humor. Tigers need to express themselves, and when they are distressed, they require affection that is transparent. To be unstable is to be unworthy of him and this never produces the desired results.

No matter how melancholy he may look, no matter how difficult the despair he finds himself in at any given moment, do not ever think he will give up.

He hates to be forgotten, and his two most outstanding defects are speed and insecurity, if he manages to find the balance, he will be a winner.

His appearance is usually attentive, innocent, and bright, that is why he gets a lot of compliments. For that reason, do not even think of mocking or criticizing him inappropriately, never forget that he has beautiful hidden nails that are always sharp.

The Tiger loves to be fashion conscious and loves to spoil himself by spending hours in shopping malls and beautifying himself in hair salons. He is super condescending and understanding with his children, qualities that give him the ability to have an excellent relationship with them.

Tigers are romantic, enthusiastic, and touchy. Both men and women are overly controlling and capable of initiating conflict when resentful.

They get along very well with the Pig, which will be the perfect seasoning for the Tiger's rages and will provide him with security. The Tiger will have a particularly good friendship with the Dog, which is not only able to tame him, but also to make him reflect. The Horse will also be an excellent partner for the Tiger, since they coincide in many concepts of life.

The Rat, the Goat, the Rooster have no difficulty in relating to the Tiger. The association between the Tiger and the Ox, the Snake or the Monkey is not suitable.

Rabbit

Characteristics

Rabbits are prone to worry about others, and extraordinarily little about themselves. Other people's problems cause them concern since they try to help whenever possible. They are exceedingly kind and supportive. When they hear news about global problems it makes them want to send money, or create movements to change the world, but they never act.

There is the possibility of seeing them sad for ulterior motives, which they will want to share with anyone who is willing to listen. If they are educated, they can be excellent speakers, or do jobs that involve qualities such as diplomacy or politics. They can be moved by the feelings of others, and by reading a book they can identify with its characters in a profound way. For this reason, they are particularly good counselors, and their friends admire their tenderness.

They have a marked tendency to idealize others and think that they will receive the same as they give, that is why they can suffer disappointments and unexpected breakups. Rabbits should reflect that some relationships are not forever, accept the defects of others as something inevitable, since no one is perfect.

Although they long to be happy, and to live in peace, their exasperated search for these virtues can be frustrated by their tendency to evade reality. Nevertheless, they can overcome conflicts like no other sign, as they are used to suffering disappointments and failures.

Rabbits are creative and meticulous. Their penetrating intelligence and negotiating skills ensure a promotion in any job. Despite their docile identity, Rabbits have an uncommon self-assurance.

He achieves his goals because of his determination, and although at times he may seem to lag, that is due to his sense of caution. While everyone else is anxious to get to the end of the road, the Rabbit thinks that tomorrow everything will go on just the same. In short, the Rabbit knows how to live and is willing to let others live. Mentally they will not forget any detail, neither your mistakes nor your successes. But if what they value is not so difficult, nor definitive, they will let it go. This characteristic makes him loved and popular. Neither think that the Rabbit goes out to fight for you, that is to ask him too much. He can lend you money, but no more than that. And if you happen to be excessively annoying you can bet that he will look for a way to elegantly disappear from your life.

A Rabbit that has not evolved, will be imaginative in excess, hypersensitive or cold. He will hate to share suffering, security will be his obsession, and he will avoid dangerous situations. He will flee from conflicts by appearing insensitive or fearful. The preference in his life will be his subsistence, and he will not believe that others can take care of him.

In general, Rabbits recover easily from crises, and although they are fragile, their tenacity appears at the right moment. They are very agreeable, and for that reason they enjoy many things that for others go unnoticed. Rabbits are compatible with Goats, with whom they share a love for tangible well-being.

It will also have a good relationship with the Dog, or the Pig. But it will not support the vanity, nor the censures of the Rooster, nor will it be frightened by the Tiger, which it will avoid just like the Horse.

Dragon

Characteristics:

Understanding a person of the Dragon sign is a bit tricky. This animal possesses the ability to persuade anyone who is not very perceptive, but it will cause him to make himself believed if his audience has a conventional mental faculty. For that reason, he gets lonely occasionally. The Dragon enjoys this quality of being different and relies on it to escape social engagements.

Friends have a wonderful time with him, as he is spontaneous, and you can never imagine what he is going to do next. They are self-employed and try not to need anyone at work. That is why you will find them starting their own business and developing it with insightful ideas.

The Dragon always thinks he is right and even if he is wrong, for him it will have been a frustrated attempt, obligatory in the circuit of evolution towards a greater progress, which will provide him not to be wrong again.

Some people will be enraptured and obey the Dragon's orders, others will loathe it and try to set traps to see it fall, and others will perceive it as a rare specimen from afar, without approaching it.

Other signs do not know how to proceed with the Dragon, but Dragons have learned, due to their intelligence, to act in diverse ways, to accommodate others. This skill is not possessed by all Dragons. The generality tends to be as they are, since they think that to force their way of being is to waste energy uselessly and that those who really must adapt are the others, and not them.

It is possible that, although the Dragon possesses a shrewd intelligence, sometimes he does not realize many things, which are on a human level, such as double intentions, and all those human qualities with a tendency to cheating and perversity. For that reason, Dragons may suffer critical moments in their relationships in general.

Although Dragons love beauty, they tend to last only a brief time in passion, if ever Cupid arrows them. They immediately look for another partner with whom to enjoy fleeting moments of passion. Only a shrewd and subtle partner like the Dragon can woo him.

They are not jealous, because they have never had reason to be. And if their partner is unfaithful, they take it philosophically. They look for new experiences in their partners, and as soon as the person does not offer anything new, they start looking for someone else.

Between the Monkey and the Dragon there is an unavoidable attraction, as both succumb fascinated by the external qualities of the other. The Dragon and the Rat make an unbreakable combination, as the Rat's mischievousness will replace the Dragon's innocence, while the Dragon's power will help the Rat's impotence.

The Snake helps to calm the slips provoked by the impulse of the Dragon and brings the firmness so that this one enjoys its intelligence when it knows how to stop to reflect. The Tiger, the Rooster, the Horse, the Goat, the Rabbit, and the Pig will ask the Dragon to protect them and share their goods with them.

Two Dragons can get along well if they connect as an invulnerable whole, anticipating that they should not rival each other so as not to crush each other, and nullify each other's capabilities.

Snake

Characteristics

The Snake has paranormal or psychic faculties. The well-known sixth sense, allows Snakes to sense risks and take blind risks with new plans, merely because they have had a hunch.

The Snake is perceptive and can clarify the difficult acts of humans. That is the reason we find psychologists, mediums, and parapsychologists among people of this sign.

Snakes know how to help those in need if it does not affect their bank account. Sometimes they exhibit tendencies to materialism, and although they are not greedy, they find it difficult to be detached. She tends to save excessively, and then fails to find the proper use for that money because the thought of spending alone causes her anxiety. Nevertheless, she likes to gamble in some games, since she was born with a star.

They are possessive in love, and cannot stand being cheated on by their partner, which is why they are jealous. Snakes are conceited, they are particularly good lovers and enjoy being carried away by the dominance of another person in a quiet way. They are serene and hate surprises. They are condescending to themselves but are extremely hard when it comes to making demands on others.

Snakes love abundance and being surrounded by beauty. For this reason, many Snakes seek mates with economic status.

A Snake is unlikely to have money problems, since it gets what it needs at the right time. If by chance she suffers a major monetary loss, this circumstance will not be repeated because the Snake assimilates nimbly. She can remedy shortfalls with extraordinary speed and is very sensible in negotiations.

When a Snake is filled with rage and fury, his resentment knows no bounds, his furtive and taciturn hostility remains intensely rooted. Her anger will reveal itself more in a humiliation, than in a violent quarrel. She is always one step ahead of any suspicion and has the power to wait for the exact moment for a revenge.

As for the partner, she is guided by her own rules. She enjoys power, and all that it symbolizes, including obviously money, and if she cannot get it herself, she will marry whoever possesses it or partner.

Regardless of how prosperous, or needy your partner is, she will become your source of capital. And if by any chance he or she has not achieved a prominent place, but possesses the skills, the Snake will push him or her to success. She will study what is necessary, and will proceed as an admirable magistrate, without ceasing to indicate him or her shrewdly every occasion that reveals itself to him or her on the way.

All Snakes have an extensive sense of humor. In difficulties, the Snake always produces a joke that lifts the spirits. Even in the worst of difficulties, the Snake will never fail to use that spark.

The best relationships for the Snake are with the Ox, Rooster, and Dragon. They also form a good combination with the Rat, Rabbit, Goat and Dog.

It should be far from the Tiger who may not appreciate its shrewdness. The Horse is a vulgar relation, and the Monkey's mischievousness will challenge the Snake's discernment.

Between two Snakes there can be a peaceful harmony, but with the Pig they have nothing in common.

Horse

Characteristics

The Horse is impulsive as it rushes towards its goals without thinking. It is as if he has never had difficulties or dealt with obstacles, because of his ability to fail and not lose his desire to succeed.

They are charming, prone to talk without thinking. The Horse at a social gathering makes everyone laugh, and the poisoned faces of those present do not worry him since he only has time to think of himself and achieve his goals. However, he does not do it with bad intentions, since his attitudes are the result of lack of good sense and maturity, and if he perceives that he made a mistake he has the capacity to apologize and repent from his heart.

Horses do not like to be dependent, and if by chance in their work they must tolerate a boss, they have an extremely tough time. They detest the laws of individuals who they assume have worse class than him, even if these people have superior positions. For that reason, he will always try to be a professional who works independently, owner of his own business.

Although the Horse loves to be appreciated, he is convinced of how masterful his work is. Sometimes this evidence blinds him, believing that he can confuse others, just by showing off in front of their eyes.

They like to feel free; home is not a concept that synchronizes with their ideas, and although they are happy with it and always find jobs that entertain them, they miss going out with friends and going to parties. He likes to change, challenges and dangers. If by chance he is offered an unstable job, but one that gives him the facility to climb the ladder quickly and increase his social status, he will jump at it without thinking.

In love, his resolutions push him to choose partners that do not suit him, he may fall in love with someone who lives in another country, or with someone who is engaged.

Despite that, they desire stability in a dull life, therefore, the partner who will support them will be the one who knows how to find the balance between a boring life, and a few escapes to the hidden. Undoubtedly, they are cheerful and use their power of attraction to get what they need.

On the negative side, the Horse is impetuous and dangerous. He usually forgets his misfortunes quickly, but this will cause him to lose admiration within his circle of friends. He also occasionally exerts fierce coercion when people do not get what he wants. The Horse delivers little compared to what he demands, becoming fundamentally selfish when it comes to his attention.

Sometimes he is generous with money, not restricting it as much as he does with his energies, which he wants always to fit for his purposes.

The Horse daily makes friends in whom he will place his trust half-heartedly and which he will leave as soon as he is annoyed, to appear as if nothing had happened when he wishes. They are sensitive, but if they get angry, they will not hesitate to cause pain with their words.

If you absolutely love a Horse, do not confine him. Enthusiastic and unbridled, they have tempestuous relationships that do not end well. Only when they grow up, and very much to their regret, they will assume their commitments.

Luck can accompany them with money in different periods of their life, but that does not assure their future since they are bad at managing their economy. They will confess that they do not care about that, but they really trust in their luck, and they know that something or someone will always save them.

They are dramatic and tell lies, which, of course for them are merciful, as this helps them to persuade others, from whom they will run away before accepting advice.

 The Tiger, the Dog and the Goat will be your best relationships on the road in all areas. You may also have magical moments with the Dragon, Snake, Monkey, Rabbit, Pig, Rooster, or other Horse.

For the Rat, the Horse is too wild and unstable. Neither does the Ox accept the Horse's discrepancies, and his creativity, rather than a positive characteristic, seems to him to be a quality that leads him to ruin.

Goat

Characteristics

The Goat has a melancholic personality that comes to the fore when he has truly spent a long time silently enduring some kind of disloyalty. He does not complain, he has trouble expressing his emotions and therefore it is difficult for him to know what is bothering him. For that reason, he may suddenly show it in an exaggerate way. People close to him perceive warning signs when something offends them.

She is an excellent worker if not pressured, when under pressure she blocks. She feels insecure about her work if she is not encouraged or praised. She does not tolerated falsehoods, although she does not like blunt truths either. When grading her work, it is better to start with a praise and continue with a constructive reproach.

Occasionally we find them in positions of authority. When this happens, the Goat has managed to find a balance between its cavil and distrust.

In love they are affectionate, cordial and very tolerant. If she is loved properly, she can be the most wonderful partner, because the Goat when she is happy projects it to others and makes life more comfortable for those around her. However, if something makes her uncomfortable, she keeps it to herself and when you least expect it, she explodes in an annoying argument with her partner.

The Goat is very enthusiastic. They may not realize when they really want it or when it is a whim. Goats are very receptive to displays of affection and have the capacity to love someone who gives them the slightest hint of romance.

Being sad and not managing her emotions is her most negative side. Another of her flaws is that she goes overboard in her spending, squandering money as if it were not hers.

The Goat is sympathetic to others, does not tolerate criticism, its moods are changeable, and it is subjective.

The Goat has fantastic luck, people often give her money or leave her an inheritance. The Goat never forgets birthdays, or any other special occasion, because she is very traditional.

Setbacks drive her so mad that she is unable to overcome them.

When it comes to aesthetics, the Goat will not deceive you because it has a fine and elegant taste and peculiarities. But do not forget that it also loves to spend a lot and that it is not practical. If you have as ascendant a sign like the Dragon, the Snake, or the Tiger, it is not advisable that you do jobs that require excessive responsibility.

Anything grotesque discourages her. It is so sensitive to harmony that its mood depends on its surroundings. The Goat works best in airy and charmingly ornamented environments. It needs the support of dynamic and honest people.

The Horse, Pig and Tiger have cheerful characteristics that will improve the Goat's temperament. It will also agree well with the Rabbit, Monkey, Dragon, Rooster, Snake, and with another Goat.

Monkey

Characteristics

The Monkey is the sign that provokes the most arguments. Some see him as someone perceptive and very jovial, others catalog him as insolent and libertine, meanwhile his partner will live hypnotized of having conquered the most enthusiastic being in the universe. His way of being adapts him eruditely to the environment where he is, and he will know how to proceed as required in any circumstance. However, if he feels comfortable, he may start to be the clown of the party, and even hurt someone's feelings with his solid polemics. The Monkey has little concern for the feelings of others, as he does not usually understand them well.

In an argument it is preferable to ignore him, because if you try to make him reason it will be in vain. It is convenient to learn from his skills to be able to successfully get out of disputes.

In love it is exceedingly rare for them to fall madly in love. They prefer the other to fall in love, their passions are ephemeral. They desire more a one-night stand than the responsibilities of home, if by chance they get married, it will be after a series of agreements or having stumbled upon someone like him.

Monkeys are stubborn and always have a solution to the problems they face. Starting a business with them, although exhausting, is a clever idea as they will bring everything they know and possess to make it succeed. It is this ability to succeed that makes them very competent for success, which is why they are at the bottom one day and at the top the next.

Their power of persuasion makes them excellent politicians, salespeople and really any goal they set for themselves. The Monkey has no respect for others or has an excess of self-respect, they are self-serving, cocky, and conceited, competitive, and very skilled at hiding their emotions while inventing their subtle misdeeds.

Anyone who knows the Monkey well will find it exceedingly difficult not to admire his lust for life, that quality sets him apart from others and for that reason he is often envied. The Monkey's reputation can be as shaky as a pendulum, but nevertheless, he never projects an image of being overly concerned about what others think of him because in his mind he is sure that he can change their minds.

This does not indicate that he is apathetic or repels criticism. On the contrary, the Monkey abides by fairness. But you must be aware because the only thing he always considers are his own beliefs. His touches of grace are disastrous, but when one recovers one must accept that he has never been defeated with such elegance and subtlety. The worst thing is that there is a chance that he will wrap you up again, and that you will fall under the charm of his charisma because in the end you become fond and fond of him.

The Monkey not only possesses an excellent memory, but is also practical, and never wastes time on things, or people for pleasure. Each Monkey is unique, no two are alike, and although he is full of faults, people enjoy his company because they cannot despise his dexterity and wiles. The cunning of the Monkey is famous, when he loses the Monkey is not capricious because when the destiny is not in his favor, he gives in.

In short, the Monkey is an affectionate and affable person, who is determined to work vigorously. He usually achieves what he desires without trying, and for this reason he quickly becomes disinterested in what he has achieved. He must practice tolerance and constancy, otherwise no one will ever trust him.

 The Dragon loves his company because of his good judgment, and the Rabbit, the Goat, the Dog, the Horse, and the Ox will favor the Monkey's mobility and will appreciate his ability and competitiveness. The Rooster and the Pig need your intelligence.

With its suspicious mind, the Snake will never be totally at ease with the Monkey. The Tiger is the prime target of his mischief and mischief. When they clash the Monkey displays his bravery and knowing that the Tiger does not like to lose, he will rejoice in overwhelming him.

Rooster

Characteristics

The Rooster is vain, but with a heart of gold. He shows off with dignity and behaves at the level of someone who deserves respect and consideration. He is a persevering worker, follows the rules and does not like to get mixed up in gossip. If there is extra work to be done, he does it without protest because he hates to leave things half done. Their capacity for abstraction and quietness makes them very competent for intellectual work.

They spend their money on luxuries because they like to live comfortably. We can say that they are not very frugal, but they are not austere either. Let us say they are capricious.

The Rooster is a good lover in every sense of the word. He is sentimental and expects the same in return. He likes to look seductive and takes great care of his physical appearance for the moments when he will meet his partner. Within his behavior patterns infidelity has no place since he aspires to find his soul mate, someone to share his life with.

Roosters love to communicate because in this way they can show that they are informed and intelligent. This ability also includes writing. He is very jovial, insightful, and entertaining, and loves to recount his adventures.

The Rooster that manifests its negative side is self-serving, mocking, and bellicose. He thinks he is always right and has no self-confidence.

Sometimes he likes to be flattered and suffers from delusions of grandeur.

El Gallo is a great economist of other people's finances, if by any chance you have economic problems due to your lack of control with money, give your finances to El Gallo. You will see that in the blink of an eye he will give you a straight calculation.

If you want to play a Rooster you must admit and reason that he loves controversy, and this for him is simple mental gymnastics. Even if it is embarrassing, you must understand that there is nothing particular about his behaviors and persevere outside the battle line once you understand that he eternally has an arsenal to defend himself.

The Rooster when they have a lot of money will be generous only to their family, or at some point they want to earn the devotion of their admirers. For that reason, keep in mind that the only free thing you can get from a Rooster is his advice.

Nevertheless, with all his faults, the Rooster is honest in his desire to support others and has good intentions in everything he initiates.

With his varied faculties and his enthusiasm for work, the Rooster will start incredibly young and will achieve success in life at an early age. What he will really need to obtain is measure in everything he starts. It does not convince him to accept his mistakes and that makes him hurt any person, and even denigrate his enemies. It is not convenient to minimize your influences, since with your professional sense you can achieve tremendous triumphs if you set your mind to it.

The Rooster makes an excellent pair with the Snake and the Ox. The Dragon will find delight in the Rooster's future goals. The Tiger, the Goat, the Monkey, and the Pig will be good partners for the Rooster.

Two Roosters together will get a legitimate Rooster feud. The Rooster will always have conflicts with the Rat and the Rabbit.

The relationship of the Dog with the Rooster will alternate between normal and spoiled. They can work together, but they are not designed to share a family life.

Dog

Characteristics

Dogs love to make other people happy, although often their stubbornness and way of interpreting things with an excess of legality can stimulate conflicts. They think the world is upside down, although they do not try to transform it, they just adapt to it.

Dogs are extremely faithful. Their faithfulness is demonstrated in friendship, and love, although that does not mean that they are extraordinary lovers. Dogs may experience enthusiastic moments, but they will be only that, as they tend to be afflicted by mundane situations that accept more space in their mind than their work, friends, or partner. Even if they do not love enough, they will always try to save relationships because they have particularly good feelings and will do their best to help. They will always solve other people's problems before they happen. Some may interpret this as meddling, and their stubbornness will prevent them from reasoning that their desire to help sometimes proves embarrassing to others.

Dogs are good advisors and follow orders from their superiors. Their nature helps to ameliorate any conflict within a company. This, together with their peculiar sense of equality, qualifies them for social work.

It is rare for the Dog to get annoyed with someone, he will make him reason, without hating him. Not all Dogs seek conflict; on the contrary, they aim to protect humanity and the common good. Once a Dog makes the decision to accept a just cause, he always triumphs because his efforts and values are high. Dogs are very responsible, they are mediators by temperament and will listen to your argument with interest, but if you ask them to tell you about their life, they will be elusive and discreet.

The Dog sometimes has a bad reputation for being sarcastic, but that is a generality. For him there are no tapestries, it is either black or white. Nothing can be halfway. He needs to know how you behave before he can be comfortable with you.

Comfortable, determined and possessing a precise affluence, the Dog will be a good counselor who will not show mercy, not even to himself.

People trust Dogs for their discretion and sense of duty, but this does not cancel out their tendency to provoke the petty quarrels to which they are so prone. Although always satisfied and pleased, the Dog is melancholic by instinct. He tends to fret for no reason, and always needs to give concise answers. When angry he can be unpleasant or anxious, but in general he is serene and willing to meet the needs of others around him.

Once you win the loyalty of a Dog, he will put all his trust in you and provide you with absolute support. People of this sign are energetic and can take a lot of worry without going broke. The Dog's best compatibility is with the Horse, the Rabbit, and the Tiger.

It will never have complications with the Rat, the Snake, the Monkey, the Pig or with another Dog.

However, it is exceedingly difficult for a Dog to deal with a Rooster, and he will never be able to give all his trust to the Dragon. His relationship with the Goat is not healthy.

Pig

Characteristics

If the Pig were not so honest, he would keep more friendships, or he would not lose so many opportunities and suitable contacts. Pigs believe that truth is primarily, so broken relationships are no more disturbing to them than having a relationship based on openness.

The uncertainty that the Pig projects is the result of an enormous preoccupation. They must meditate on everything a hundred times, and even when they decide on something, they doubt whether choosing another path would have been more convenient.

Despite all these uncertainties, when they decide, they find it hard to make a change and choose to continue the path with determination.

Pigs are accommodating, condescending, and fair. Their attitudes make them well suited for labor, as well as jobs where concentration is paramount.

In love they will be faithful, accommodating, and affable. Although they have a profound sense of humor, and know how to enjoy life, in relationships they should not be associated with individuals who are very communicative, or who are attracted to fun, as they enjoy the home life, and will prefer gatherings with close friends Rather than with crowds.

Holder of great integrity, he is not dazzled by working on more than one thing at a time, but this does not limit him to go after the dynamic experiences of jouissance, which in its erroneous version could be its destruction.

The Pig is not attracted to be the boss, for that reason he is a loyal companion who will never compete to be the focus of attention, although sometimes he will be so without considering it by his actions, becoming indispensable.

Charitable and honest, he is lucky and never lacks a faithful friend who is determined to help him if he needs it. However, he chooses to provide Rather than require.

Although he is very easily outraged, he quickly renounces hostility because he chooses to be in harmony, which makes him complacent and resigned to cooperate and listen to any argument. He loves to do charitable works, he is not impressed by obligations, and it is as if he was born to fight against them.

Its negative side, if he decides to expose it, is that he can be kind to take advantage of a certain situation and thus without qualms dispose of anything as if it were his.

If he falls in love, he is devoted to his love and fidelity without asking for anything in return. He puts passion and happiness in all his actions, making his partner feel the navel of the world. He is very sensual, and does not know how to hide his emotions, nor deny the claims of the person he loves, giving himself to dark passions.

The Pig is not a good leader and supervisor, and in turn it irritates him to find himself limited in his ambitions. This makes him selfish and useless. His indestructible propensity to give expresses his great obligation to cooperate. He likes to live in the present and tries not to travel into the past, nor to anticipate the future, which is why he possesses a great power of rehabilitation and an iron determination in the face of the tribulations of daily life.

Strongly meticulous, he does not rest if he stumbles into formal disputes and even if he is reasonable, he will feel that he caused the problem by not having had the ability to preserve harmony.

The Rabbit and the Goat are his favorite accomplices because they share with him the need for serenity and harmony. The Tiger accompanies him on winding roads. The Rat, the Ox, the Horse, the

Rooster, the Dog, and the Dragon share joyful opportunities with the Pig.

Another Pig, it is not a pleasant association, nor entertaining, but it will not work badly. The hardest oppositions are with the Snake and the Monkey, since it always loses with these two malicious little animals.

Characteristics of the Signs according to their Element

Rat

Wood Rat

Wood Rats are poor during childhood, although well-nourished and well-groomed in middle age.

Men can have a free life but suffer some distressing experience due to problems with their family and conflicts with siblings.

Women are exemplary and intelligent, both in their profession and in their family life.

The Wood Rat does not do well in relationships with powerful people, although they are highly revered for their sense of freedom, which generates both beneficial and detrimental results. The negative consequences are that they are unlikely to get a promotion. The positive effect is that they will be able to have a balanced family life without worrying about food and clothing.

They are always well educated about regulations, follow traditional models of integrity, and have a spectacular sense of teamwork, get along well with the people around them, although they sometimes project a selfish image. They have a charming way of treating everyone they meet in their path and are ready to serve and help others without asking for anything in return.

They have stable values and use tactics with docility to achieve their ends. They love to feel protected, yet they often find themselves beset by a jolt of anguish, which is why they work hard every day of their lives.

Fire Rat

Fire Rats are immensely powerful, and brave to face any problem, or eventuality.

They are kind and loyal to their friends, but extremely strict with themselves. They have sharp tongues; therefore, they can often embarrass other people. They are silent but will express what they know bluntly when they could talk.

They have deep bonds of connection with their parents, are affectionate with their siblings, and place infinite value on their family. They are willing to make a lifelong effort for their loved ones to live in well-being. They fall blindly in love and are ready to do anything for their partner without complaining, even if the love is arbitrary. The Fire Rat is creative and energetic, ready to complete any project, especially an innovative and appealing one. They have an insightful and surprising mentality, the faculty to make conclusive forecasts and, thanks to their inquiries, they always make great discoveries. Their talent for surviving in any habitat, finding the right solutions, and setting goals gives them certainty in the future. If this Rat would overcome its predisposition to litigation and gossip, a peaceful and constant life would be guaranteed.

This mischievous and active Rat is mesmerized by taking part in all kinds of functions and is comfortable fighting for equality and healthy living. They are attracted to exploring and fashionable clothes. They are outspoken, but provocative by nature. However, they are the most giving of all Rats.

Although they are enterprising and altruistic, they do not seek to display great cunning and, at times, dramatize in the dispute for fame.

Earth Rat

Earth Rats are cordial, dignified, tolerant, humble, and capable. They are very formal at work and are always supported for their good connections.

They have a deep-rooted sense of self-esteem, sometimes their new friends misunderstand them, however, they later transform into stable friendships when the mistake is clarified.

In their profession they should study more so that they can get benefits. They should take more care of their family instead of participating in so many social events, this is the only way they will strengthen their marital bond.

Its inadequacies are disguised by its innumerable qualities, consequently, it is esteemed, appreciated, and adored. This Rat will opt for the harder, but safer route. Sometimes the uncertainty makes it delay in taking decisions for that sometimes it suffers enormous mishaps. Boldness and efficiency are lacking in the Earth Rat.

An Earth Rat is sensible, and happiness is lived with discipline. It is balanced and invulnerable to false expectations. They are always diplomatic and loyal to friends, and their friendships last a long time. This Rat has an incredible capacity for concentration and is accustomed to doing its work diligently.

Among her shortcomings, we find that she sometimes concentrates more on the result, that she thinks she is doing everything right, and does not pay attention to others, especially if she is in a hurry to finish the job and wants everything to be exactly as she says.

This Rat is very restless when it comes to its popularity, but it is tender and always helps its relatives. It has great material demands and always contrasts its earnings with those of its friends. It is often exaggerated, and ambitious for money. The Earth Rat hates to take risks and for that reason misses good opportunities.

Metal Rat

The Metal Rat is intelligent and jealous, and they always do things by halves. They are remarkably close to their parents and siblings and are perceptive and subtle.

They have an extraordinarily keen sense of conscience, but never recognize their faults. They are overly sensitive and attach immense importance to their individual experiences.

This Metal Rat likes to be seen by others. They are communicative and have an innate ability to convince others, and their grace disguises their jealousy.

They idolize money but are not good at saving it like the other Rats of the other elements. They would be more successful if they controlled their possessive instinct.

The Metal Rat is very sincere and exclusive. She is ready to work at any time. It is not worth arguing with her, because her criteria are very solid.

This prototype of Rats is idealistic, but they are emotional. Sometimes they can hide their emotions, manifesting pleasantness, and politeness. They are often suspicious and materialistic, and struggle to acquire a positive appraisal from the people around them. Metal Rats are money lovers, but they are not stingy, they are not interested in squandering a hefty sum of money on what they think is valuable and of quality. Metal Rats are very skilled at investing money.

The Metal Rat's home will always be luxuriously appointed. They often have exclusive taste, and value tradition and splendor. If this Metal Rat uses its qualities, it will gain popularity and love from others. This Metal Rat will persevere to integrate into circles of influential people.

Water Rat

Water is a representation of life and fertility, but it also manifests itself in the form of ice blowing a lethal cold.

If the phlegmatic water side of the Water Rat excels, they become cold and ruthless. They have almost no enthusiasm because they are calculating. This Rat is moody when relating to other people.

The judicious and calm character of this type of Rat allows them to gain the friendship of people close to them. A wonderful ability of this Rat is its ability to calm down any offender and prevent dangerous scenarios. This makes the Rat not fearful and violent.

These Rats can be found in any profession, as they do not tremble in the face of problems and difficulties that may come their way. They are truly cold-blooded and protect the social interests of the public, along with their own interests and motivations.

Water Rats must learn to be quicker to decide, as this is the only way to break down the wall of ice with which they often protect themselves. Therefore, fighting to show others their true essence is something that deserves the effort. In addition, your seriousness, precision, and clarity can easily convince that you have made an adjustment.

A talent and sharp congenital focus, as well as an enthusiastic yearning for discernment, make this lineage of Rats the most insightful among other individuals.

Ox

Wooden Ox

People born under the sign of the Wood Ox are impatient and always ready to defend the defenseless. They can care for their friends with selflessness in times of hardship. Nothing prevents them from offering flattery, and because of their upright character, they earn many enemies. Freedom-loving and independent, they cannot tolerate being cooped up for long, and their friends and loved ones must respect their need for freedom of movement. An incurable optimist, he has big dreams, and hopes for the future, and is always pursuing some end.

He has great faith and confidence in life, and failures do not defeat his spirit. He always recovers from his disappointments, often with another dream or project. He has a playful and sporting attitude towards life, and a philosophical attitude towards his own mistakes. She perceives future trends, can project the whole picture, and likes to theorize and speculate. Because she does not take herself too seriously, she often does not realize how much her candid comments can hurt. In fact, even if she does not realize it, her insensitivity and lack of understanding for the feelings of others is one of her worst faults.

She has good mental focus, and the ability to become immersed in her work. Seems to know things on an instinctive, non-verbal level and prefers to learn through direct experience or apprenticeship Rather than through books or lectures.

Water Ox

This Ox is very secretive. Does not trust anyone with their business plans, so as not to interfere with their implementation. Able to predict the course of events, to avoid disruptions and problems. Since these qualities are complemented by exceptional honesty and the ability to clearly express their thoughts and sociability, these Oxen are priceless in politics and social activities. As a rule, people born in the year of the Water Ox love wives and idolize children.

A thoughtful, practical, and prohibitively ambitious Water Ox demonstrates a subtle mind and strict principles. He uses things for his purposes and calculates his every step. He always knows what to do with himself and how to organize his activities.

This Ox is more intelligent and flexible compared to other types of Oxen. He is ready to accept recommendations, but rarely agrees to change anything or apply uncomfortable methods of work or leisure activities. But he will not be indignant if he is advised to change his tactics a little, especially if he believes that this will lead him to achieve his goal. He is concerned about his social status and security; in most cases, he observes law and order in everything he undertakes.

It will contribute to the common cause, working well together with everyone. He can easily manage his life, unless, of course, he is too weak or does not require too much from life and other people. He can concentrate on several goals at once and can break all counterarguments with his usual indestructible calmness, attentiveness, and firmness.

Intimacy is not easy for this Ox, and he may appear to be a cold or insensitive person because of his extreme caution and emotional reserve. Due to separations or painful relationships early in his life, he does not initially trust others and it takes him a long time to remove his barriers. He thinks he has few friends or people who appreciate him. Needs to learn to value and love himself more, and to learn to express his appreciation for others more openly.

Earth Oxen

Earth Oxen are honorable and sensible, with a high sense of commitment that sets them apart from other Oxen. They attach immense importance to the balanced distribution of favors when helping others. They have an accurate appreciation of their own person, recognizing both their advantages and disadvantages. They never promise in vain, nor do they act beyond their ability. They strive to keep their promises and succeed.

They are grateful for favors received, they know how to organize and manage their work efficiently. They are cautious, making sure that they will always succeed with the help of their friends.

The Earth Ox is frugal and judicious. He tries to achieve the maximum reward in his work, being able to cheat in order not to lose. He does not limit himself in telling the truth personally, for which he is admired. They address him because they know that when the Ox speaks it is because he has a judicious proposition. This Ox usually needs to be accompanied by relations who will help him to be more affable.

This Ox is stubborn, but a little less creative than the other Oxen, being devoted to his dreams. He is reflective about his inadequacies and restrictions from an early age. He will succeed in any job he chooses, as he is a skilled person and is willing to pay the price for victory. He spontaneously shares with others and helps his friends.

Although he is sentimentally dry and insensitive, he can love sincerely overall and is very loyal to his loved ones. He will struggle tenaciously to perfect his life, and if he gets distressed, he never complains.

His power to focus and make decisions allows the Earth Ox to soar high, and never give in to any obstacle. He is the slowest, but most persuasive of the Oxen.

Fire Ox

Individuals belonging to the Fire Ox are petty and have a narrow mentality. They favor themselves for possessing knowledge but are sensitive to stimuli from the outside world due to their lack of decision-making skills. All of this can be seen in their lives, with the most common being that they often separate or divorce.

They are very severe with their partners, and their love appears and disappears easily, for that reason it is very convenient for them to be associated with communicative and dynamic people. Only people of the sign of the Rat - Water can maintain a lasting romantic relationship with them.

This Ox is a warrior, there are no obstacles or impossible paths for him. Speed is one of his most outstanding qualities and doing everything accurately and efficiently puts him at the top. His mentality, assertiveness, and modesty make him an effective guide. He does not possess an infinity of friends, but the few he has, he dedicates his life to them.

This Fire Ox should learn to listen to the opinions of his family members, because they will always give him intelligent advice.

These Oxen are sometimes impulsive, becoming more concerned with power than with other things. Fire increases the Ox's ability to control itself and create a decisive behavior.

This Ox can be more energetic and vainer than other Oxen, excluding the Metal Ox, which often prevails over the Fire Ox in these characteristics. The Fire Ox is selfish, and often subject to delirium.

Metal Ox

The Metal Element Ox is highly respected because of their excellent relationships. They are prosperous and distinguished from an early age, live comfortably in middle age, and enjoy a pleasant life in old age.

They should be careful not to get together with people who are engaged or have love triangle type romances. Those who are already engaged must learn to respect each other, or they will have marital difficulties, such as a third party who may get in the way of the relationship.

This Metal Ox has a rigid character, there is nothing and no one who can make him deviate from the path he thinks is the right one. He never acts in vain and will always get the right result in everything he sets out to do.

Metal Oxen are the most affable of all Oxen, they love to share with their friends, recreate, and be relaxed. They are good to their family and provide them with a dignified life. If this Ox were not so selfish, they would have a faster career advancement.

This Metal Ox frequently disagrees with everyone who disagrees with him, including his bosses, and anyone who dares to criticize him will feel the brunt of his anger very sharply.

Although by nature this Ox is not sophisticated, he can love art, music, and be disciplined. He has a supreme sense of responsibility, and you can take his word for it, because he does not waste words for the sake of it.

Sometimes he tries to run things over, and it can get dangerous. The Metal Ox by itself looks like an army of men when it pretends to succeed.

Tiger

Metal Tiger

Metal Tigers attach immense importance to their family life, because they love to live in peace and harmony. They are very enthusiastic, yet hesitant, and stubborn, therefore, their inner world is different from what they appear to be.

Metal Tigers know that work is important, but they never mix it with family matters. They are not expressive, and you will rarely hear them say cloying words. Despite this they are very touchy and tolerant of their partner.

Their biggest obstacle is that they never listen to advice from others, even though they really need it. They are magnetized with power and will achieve remarkable success in government work if they work with passion.

The Metal Tiger is friendly with their colleagues, and as a result, they can get a career where they can flow because of that support received.

The Metal Tiger is a great researcher, he is very affable, perspicacious, and persevering, not paralyzed by anything until he achieves his purpose. But if something goes wrong, he becomes very furious. Nevertheless, patience can save Metal Tigers from many setbacks.

The Metal Tiger is very talkative. He always likes to be active, sometimes with a bad temper. Although he tries to maintain an impressive image, he is individualistic and vain, loves competition and can work tenaciously if he is enthusiastic.

Water Tiger

The Water Tiger has a peculiar ability to assimilate new things, and they are experts in the fields of art.

They have a high sense of self-esteem, and almost never accept the recommendation of others. Despite this, they are unlikely to fail, which often attracts envy.

Water Tigers will accomplish more in their lives if they would be gracious enough to ask their friends for help. They should be cautious in making significant decisions and dealing with life's emergencies. They should not be so trusting, or they will suffer great disappointments.

Water Tigers are cordial, with a tenacious mind and Rational thinking, they love the unexplored. They do not lose their temper easily, even in difficult circumstances because they have incredible clarity of thought. When something happens that takes them out of their rhythm, they do not rush and plan their thoughts in a calculated and cold way, which increases their self-esteem.

Sincere and always willing to accept new ideals and lessons, the Water Tiger has the gift of looking at everything impartially. Water mitigates the Tiger's character by giving him the ability to see clearly where the truth is, and where the deception is.

This Tiger is sensitive to the feelings of others. Their refined intuition and shrewdness in approaching others offers them the opportunity to successfully study professions related to journalism or public relations.

This is a realistic Tiger, knows how to control his emotions and is receptive to other people's emotions. He does business in a specialized way, is rarely wrong, and is an excellent preacher. His mental skills are privileged compared to the average. Like other Tigers, he often procrastinates. He is less impulsive than other Tigers because he knows how to control his impulse.

Wooden Tiger

Wood Tigers are communicative and like to work in teams to achieve collective purposes. They can use their own intelligence and make the right decisions whenever they set their minds to it.

However, they usually only pay attention to the superficial part of a situation, and rarely delve into its principles, all of which results in missed opportunities.

Wood Tigers are always actively performing tasks beyond their capabilities, which sometimes ends in failure and disappointment. It is highly recommended that they learn from the wisdom of others to avoid stumbling at work.

The Wood Tiger has a particularly good temperament, is humorous, and very funny. This Tiger easily gets involved in the problems of others to help them solve them.

 It is distinguished from the other Tigers by its faculty to consent, and to consider the manifestations of the other people. It needs to have a little firmness and serenity if it wishes to obtain fruits quickly.

He is not violent like other Tigers and can be subtle. He is a perceptive leader, competent to give explanations and to direct the work to conquer the best conclusions. Despite all the above, he will sometimes avoid making commitments.

The Wood Tiger is very formal even with his entertainments. Like the other Tigers, he has little capacity for self-discipline, and should never accept more than he can digest.

He enjoys friendship and camaraderie, but needs freedom, and would not do well with a possessive, clingy and emotionally demanding partner. He is very generous, and dislikes meanness in others. Someone who shares his ideals, sense of fun and zest for life would be the perfect companion.

Fire Tiger

The Fire Tiger is optimistic, but weak when it comes to self-control, because for them the best moment is the present. They are enthusiastic, so they make a lot of mistakes.

Fire Tigers are very autonomous and never give in to earthly obstacles or problems. No one can imagine what they think because of their vagabond lifestyle.

The Fire Tiger is a natural guide in any profession, he is witty and cheerful, always ready to contaminate everyone with his inexhaustible energy. He is confident in his skills, assiduously does only what appeals to him, and if that does not work, he does not feel fear, he is not disappointed, on the contrary, he continues to move forward towards his goals.

In all their objectives the Fire Tiger does not always have the support of others because they do not always understand it, and the worst thing is that they are afraid to show it.

It is difficult for the Fire Tiger to keep his excitement and high spirits in check, which is why he is always ready to act. They love to be on the move, to experience new sensations and make exciting discoveries.

 The one thing you can be sure of is that you will always be vibrant and influential. The Fire element makes the Tiger even more expressive. This Tiger can impress anyone. He knows exactly how to use his energy at work, and how to achieve his goals.

He constantly channels his intense energy and quickly puts his ideas into practice. Occasionally he is exaggeratedly dramatic. He is powerful, and decorous. He is very cheerful and hates to refuse when asked for a favor. He always has goals in his mind, and when he finishes them, he quickly starts a new objective.

Tigre de Tierra

Earth Tigers are reflective, so they can express their thoughts without problems. They are objective and balanced, with firm beliefs, and possess the potential to find the truth.

Earth Tigers concentrate on one thing at a time, and dislike taking things lightly. They are always seen differently by other people because of their magnetic aura.

The Earth Tiger is incredibly happy and famous. He is always surrounded by friends, partners, whom he is happy to serve. The Earth Tiger is serene, serious, and takes care of his prestige. They should learn to consider the opinions of others as this would make life easier for them.

This Tiger has a serene and judicious temperament. He treats people affectionately, is skillful and objective in his actions. It strives to succeed, does not rush to conclusions, and rarely loses patience. The people around him know that he is reasonable and shrewd.

The Earth element mixed with the Tiger gives you a stable personality, benefiting you with greater focus, something that allows you to work more quickly and objectively. You observe the circumstances that happen to you with an X-ray eye, and rarely allow emotions to obscure your view.

The Earth Tiger applies his talents and abilities in those areas with which he is well connected, and which can bring him substantial income.

Occasionally, the Earth Tiger is exaggerated with his pride, and insensitive, mainly when he is infatuated with something.

Rabbit

Water Rabbit

The Water Rabbit is pleasant and friendly, they adapt easily to different circumstances, however, they are easily influenced by others due to their fragile mind and values.

They are very co-dependent on the people in whom they place their trust, and often feel depression when they lose their subordination. They must learn to be independent so that they can feel real security.

Water Rabbits are seduced by unhealthy habits; therefore, it is advisable that they do not waste their money on unnecessary social gatherings but save it for tough times.

This Rabbit differs from the others in that it is shrewd, and able to listen to the judgments of others.

In his career, he succeeds because reason, alacrity, and thoroughness are in his DNA. However, he needs to be more confident, so he would do better.

This is a very delicate Rabbit, and naturally romantic. It does not support to be harassed or harassed, nor to have disputes where the opinions are unpleasant.

 It is extremely easy to put pressure on him from the outside as he experiences emotionally the afflictions of others.

Wooden Rabbit

Wood Rabbits are subtle, crafty, and good at making petty plans. They appear bold in appearance, but deep down they are very devious and often fight with their friends over frivolous things.

They are prone to precipitous changes of temperament. Nevertheless, they are devoted to love. The darkness of suffering will linger in their hearts for a long time if they fail to be with the one, they adore.

Wood Rabbits are prone to be materialistic in life and place excellent value on an impartial sharing of everything. They would have a more balanced home life and a more bearable job if they could show more respect for others.

The Wood Rabbit hates to be alone and inactive. He loves social gatherings and organizing outrageous parties. He is a faithful companion, but never pretends to share his secrets with anyone. It has a more radiant character than the other Rabbits, although it occasionally refuses to take advice because it is afraid of falling into a trap.

The Wood Rabbit is adaptable to any circumstance, can easily become part of a team because he is very diplomatic and rises slowly in his professional area. They are prone to avoid making decisions that offend someone or create a threatening precedent. This disability to act with precision and to take a specific place can demolish the popularity of the Wood Rabbit. He should be more confident and able to protect himself from those who wish to take advantage of his greatness.

Fire Rabbit

The Fire Rabbit has an insightful and tolerant mind with unique ideas. They work solemnly and were born to be leaders.

Not only do they know how to consider and utilize people, but they also know how to enable different aptitudes and bring them together to be experts in life.

The Fire Rabbit should not panic in times of unforeseen difficulties, such as lack of money. Good counselor and shrewd, he cements ties with any individual who is honest. He does not lie to his friends, and his circle is quite restricted.

Self-discipline and perception provide you with the ability to accurately dispose of your own focus. For these reasons, his instinct for self-preservation, fear, takes away the opportunity to demonstrate his abilities. There can be great benefits in this Rabbit's life if tutored by friends who will motivate him to venture out at the right time.

This Rabbit is cool, funny, and entertaining. He has a more intense personality than the other Rabbits, but he knows how to disguise his fears with the help of grace and cunning. This is a serene person. The Fire element pushes this Rabbit to be fond of enthusiastic speeches, mainly when he is not proud of something.

He is more inclined to leadership than the other Rabbits, but his techniques are Limited. Like other Rabbits, he avoids direct confrontation with his adversaries and chooses delicately devised plots.

The Fire Rabbit has good instincts and intellectual abilities. It is quick to notice any disturbance in the environment, and comfortably displays hatred and grief.

Ground Rabbit

The Earth Rabbit is very sincere, however, they project an image of bluntness to others when they are in action, so they should try to be a little more cautious.

They are very rigorous with themselves, and calculating in their career, consequently, they always move from one workplace to another. They work hard and pay attention to details, are ready to do something insubstantial, but tire quickly.

Earth Rabbits have excellent physical vitality, but their appearance is not healthy.

The Earth Rabbit is tenacious, diligent, with a well-honed sense of predicting the future outstanding. His power, talent and accuracy make him a good partner in any opportunity, especially those related to finances. Exaggerate prudence diminishes the Earth Rabbit's opportunities for fulfillment.

This is a profoundly serious Rabbit, his goals are defined, and he is very calculating in all his steps. He is careful when expressing his emotions, equanimous, and subtle. He has an objective vision of everything that surrounds him, characteristics that are primordial especially for the people superior to him.

The Earth element makes the Rabbit stable and less indulgent in its desires, although this constancy is passive. The Earth Rabbit is withdrawn and has the tendency to go deep into himself as soon as he faces a problem. He tries to maintain a harmonious rhythm with his inner world, and it is under this condition that he can act with confidence in the outer world. It never has doubts about how to use the resources it possesses to consciously resolve conflicts.

The Earth Rabbit is practical, he is constantly concerned about his well-being, sometimes being insensitive to other people's hardships if they do not agree with his own plans. Despite that, he is humble and realizes his frailties and tries to tolerate them.

Metal Rabbit

Metal Rabbits am kind, are very moderate, and detest competition. They do not like to befriend competitive or anxious people who seek instant gains.

They are bold and enthusiastic, so they have many friends from all occupations, and those who are stubborn are never friends with them.

The Metal Rabbit is quiet and clever. He knows just what he wants out of life and how he will proceed, but to others this is a total mystery. He keeps his secrets and goals with him because he is suspicious. In the circle of his relationships there are only honest people who will not subdue him with their energies. As he is cautious and prudent, he manages to climb to positions of high social status, always surrounding himself with prestigious people.

These Rabbits are very vital and have strong mental health, however, the Metal Rabbit is dependent on his powers of reflection and calculation. He is always confident that he has the right answers, and that he makes the right decisions. He patiently takes on commitments, and in his profession, he projects an unmistakable creativity.

The influence of Metal makes the Rabbit excessively preoccupied with its own aspirations and ideas. This Rabbit is more subtle than others, and ambitious. His ambitions are subordinate to his calculating mentality. The Metal Rabbit is fascinated by luxurious living and is indifferent to the opinions of others.

Dragon

Wooden Dragon

Wood Dragons are introverted and hate to talk. They are not enthusiastic about their friendships; therefore, they do not have many close friends.

Although short on personal relationships, Wood Dragons are outstanding among their peers because of their sublime manner, but this does not mean that they like to be the center of attention.

The Wood Dragon is subversive and proud. They are so appreciative of their natural strengths that they are often overly demanding. His self-confidence causes anger in others. The Wood Dragon is characterized by loyalty and constancy, but also by irritation, the most marked of all Dragons.

The Wood Dragon is a fighter, seeking sympathy from those who are like him in terms of intellectuality or social status. Apathy and foolishness drive him to despair. He is highly creative.

He actively protects his opinions and is ready to give his life for them. This Dragon is a natural fighter who does not know the term impossible.

Fire Dragon

The Fire Dragon is well liked by others. Although not all Fire Dragons are perceptive, most of them can act correctly at the right time and make the most of the opportunities that present themselves. All this brings them the benefit of many successes in their lives.

They can adapt to any situation, even if it is unstable. This Dragon is a leader par excellence who will check and evaluate everything. People who know him usually try not to disappoint him, because he always knows how to put himself in the position of others. He likes to help and advice, this attitude combined with his faithfulness, sincerity, and hard work, gives him additional benefits. Despite all these beautiful qualities, his desire to be a hermit and to isolate himself prevents him from showing his talents and abilities.

The Fire Dragon is the most gallant and cheerful of them all, he is more charmed by fighting than the other Dragons. Despite this aggressiveness, he is endowed with infinite energy and has a lot to offer to other people. He is the embodiment of supremacy, so people feel fear when they are around him.

He is a competent leader, but often wants to be treated as the King, ruining everything with his ego. Fire makes the Dragon determined and gives him the behaviors of a tyrant. The Fire Dragon squeezes others even when these people no longer have the strength to continue.

In any case, he is gentle, sincere, and impartial. His criticism tends to be objective. He can be the leader of multitudes of people, since by nature he is an architect of empires.

Earth Dragon

The Earth Dragon is insightful, insatiable, and hardworking, always looking for ways to act positively in life. However, they tend to do things by halves.

Earth Dragons have loving hearts without any trace of evil and are destined to be philanthropists.

The Earth Dragon is phenomenally successful. Not only does he achieve everything he sets his mind to, but the people around him are always ready to help him, that is, they appreciate him very much.

Earth Dragons always want the best for others. They are a bit stubborn and persistent, are always inventing a business, and often become very wealthy people.

Curious and scrupulous, they try all kinds of professions and study throughout their lives. Romantic experiences would brighten up the monotonous life of these Dragons, but they prefer to work to maintain their status.

This Dragon is characterized by intransigence, and it is absurd to expect anything else from him. However, he is fair and values the opinions of others, even if he does not agree with them. The Earth element makes him realistic, balanced and often even a little impersonal.

Although he is not as rigid as other Dragons, he loves to push people around. They are tenacious in their abilities and try to put them into practice. This Dragon knows the importance of collaboration between people and perseveres to work for the social good.

The Earth Dragon knows how to dominate himself, he loves to take the initiative, completing everything he starts without hesitation.

He is aristocratic, moderate, and unwilling to argue. However, if you denigrated his self-esteem, he would undoubtedly manifest his anger, because he demands reverence for himself.

Metal Dragon

Metal Dragons are natural, but often change their minds because their emotions change consecutively. They are unpredictable on many occasions, but do not represent harm to anyone.

They love family life, enjoy harmony, and it is especially important that they take care of their health because psychosomatic illnesses can attack them.

The Metal Dragon is mischievous and proud. They are so fond of their innate abilities that they are extremely demanding of themselves. Their self-confidence is unquestionable, but this causes displeasure in others. Metal Dragons are characterized by their righteousness and perseverance, and although they are sometimes easily irritated, they can get rid of this negative quality of their character, if they really want to.

It is the most volatile of all Dragons. He communicates well, is very explicit, and lucid, but at the same time rigid. The Metal Dragon is driven to act, is a troublemaker, and seeks the friendship of all those individuals who are like him in social status. Laziness and dullness irritate him. Metal empowers the Dragon to subdue the weakest and bend them to his will.

He is suspiciously protective of his opinions, and is ready to give his life for them, if necessary. This Dragon is a born fighter and can display a stunted aptitude of his personal courage. The Metal Dragon lacks tact and is accustomed to fighting all problems alone.

The Metal Dragon is diligent, fighting for its goals, even if that means being bold. Once it decides, it attacks and does not retreat.

Water Dragon

Water Dragons are perceptive, but lack originality, and often float with the current. Water Dragons are immensely powerful and tenacious. They always attend deftly to every detail because their goal is to make everything perfect. The only disadvantage is that they tire easily.

They are admired by their friends because of their judicious and sarcastic style, and that also earns them many romantic dates. These Dragons know how to benefit from this to find their true love.

The Water Dragon is very conforming. It does everything slowly, but in a structured way. This Dragon requires that the result be the best possible, and for that he uses all methods to achieve it.

He never misses an opportunity to succeed. He is very sociable and helpful, always admired by his friends as he possesses outstanding qualities especially for organization. He enjoys frank discussions and entertaining company.

The Water Dragon is not as powerful as others, but for the social good they can put aside their pride. They are not materialistic; they are very reserved with their things and persevere a lot because they are not as mysterious as other Dragons.

This does not mean that he is docile, on the contrary, due to his willpower, expect to see strange attitudes in this Dragon, because he loves to be true to himself.

Water placates the Dragon's energy and has a beneficial effect on him, giving him mastery of his actions and the knowledge of what is necessary to move forward with confidence.

Snake

Water Snake

Water Snakes are cunning, and active, but very affectionate. They sometimes leave their homes at a premature age, to build a decent future for themselves because of their unfortunate family background.

These Snakes value every opportunity and thrive in business because of their adventurous personalities. They will live a solid life in middle age after experiencing various difficulties.

The Water Snake should think three times before deciding what to invest its energies in, because, although they are very communicative, in various situations they change their mind.

The Water Snake is the most perceptive of all the Snakes. Her interests vary because her knowledge is universal, yet she constantly works on herself, and is always up to date. Most of the time, the Water Snake is found in culture, cosmography, and banking, where they devote themselves to divination. It has many devotees who value its virtues. It is a psychologist of people and knows how to manipulate them.

She is serene and impartial, but she is truly vengeful, and if her infinite patience runs out, be prepared for a deadly bite.

Wooden Snake

Wood Snakes place immense importance on organization, and love to live in a luxuriously decorated environment.

Wood Snakes have a talent for appreciating the arts and are super creative. Their taste is delicate, and they know how to differentiate good works from bad ones. They love to collect old things and have a talent for taking care of them.

The Wood Snake possesses outstanding qualities when compared to other Snakes. It is festive, humorous, communicative, and attentive. She is always surrounded by many friends who appreciate her wisdom and capacity for service. She also values them but does not allow anyone to invade her soul.

This Snake chooses to function alone or in a small and affable group, where everyone is equal, where no one gives orders because she hates sermons. She does not tolerate discord and conflicts.

It is the most honest Snake, with a keen wisdom and insight into the balance of power. It needs a strong mental independence and is persevering in its actions. The Wood Snake always seeks and achieves mental, emotional, and financial stability. This Snake can express its ideas firmly and can be a convincing preacher.

The Wood element makes the Snake seductive and charming. She shines like a searchlight, does not persuade others of her naivety, but tows them along with her. This Snake habitually has expensive cravings, however, because of that vanity, she may have a misconception about herself. As this Snake covets public devotion, it will go to great lengths to achieve long-term and grand triumph.

Fire Snake

Fire Snakes have experience and wisdom, think faster, and see more clearly than others, and are very talkative. They are active, and love drama. They are born to be comedians and dancers. They absolutely know how to expose their feelings in stories, although it is unusual for them to tell their private lives.

This Snake has its own opinions and is not afraid to express them. But if they bother it, it expects toxic and cruel adjectives or epithets. These things do not sit well with her appearance and demeanor. She is approachable, approachable and a good leader.

This Snake has many friends who admire it wholeheartedly for its amazing sense of humor, the ability to place a shrewd word, and suddenly prevent any mockery. The Fire Snake must learn to be flexible with other people's faults.

This Snake is vigorous, mentally, and physically. It has fire to spare, and this makes it fiery and eager. Seductive in the eyes of all, and equipped with grace, it can mesmerize anyone. She embodies self-confidence and can be a leader.

The Fire Snake can battle openly, and is by nature extraordinarily suspicious, relying only on itself. It is uncommonly quick to punish, is strong, endowed with an extravagant desire for notoriety, wealth, and power, and therefore insists on precise results.

Earth Snake

Earth Snakes know how to control their feelings because they are very reasonable. Their romantic relationships are intense, they suffer from many romantic breakups in their lives, but they can recover quickly due to their reasoning.

Earth Snakes do not like to be controlled; you should never question them. They have many possibilities to earn money, however, it is exceedingly difficult for them to save it. Sometimes they make so many mistakes that they lose sight of genuine opportunities. They should be more stable and efficient.

The Earth Snake is always oriented. It is never in a hurry, because in this way it avoids not caring. It will accomplish all tasks with accuracy and will expect much more if its work is appreciated. This Snake can be trusted in business, specifically in jobs that require accuracy and honesty.

Earth Snakes are kind-hearted and can empathize with others. She possesses many friendly friendships and is protective of her family.

It is a sincere Snake, has principles, values and is stubborn. Because of its ability to see things before others, and its congenital sinuous interests, it knows how to take charge and resolve any situation where chaos reigns. An Earth Snake is difficult to restrain and is never interested in public opinion.

This Snake is constant in her opinions and always reserves the power to choose her own decisions. She possesses an innate grace for being fashionable and knows how to use them.

Metal Snake

The Metal Snake is self-respecting, very brave, and capable, and they are surrounded by many followers from all areas of their life. Most of them have a majestic appearance, being super elegant.

These Snakes possess a lot of self-confidence and give the impression of being arrogant. They are comfortable doing everything on their own. She is a brilliant strategist, with a refined sense of when, and how to strive for profit. She is only interested in her friends and family; others are indifferent to her.

This Snake has a subtle mind, and an indomitable willpower. She is very exquisite in her tastes, correctly watching all occasions and opportunities, to take the next step. She likes to move swiftly and quietly, knows how to take a beneficial position before anyone can slow her down.

A Metal Snake always tries to get the most out of everything it finds in its life, being more prudent, ambiguous, and constant than other Snakes. This Snake knows how to get rid of its opponents, and of people who envy it.

Horse

Metal Horse

Metal Horses are sociable and are willing to help others. They are incredibly famous among their friends; however, they often insult others unintentionally due to their simplicity.

In general, they get along well with young people. Metal Horses are constant in love, but their life is full of challenges, as they have a serious and balanced relationship if their partner is prepared to put up with them.

The Metal Horse is even-tempered, decent and of values. They do everything carefully, as they detest rushing. They are revered for their politeness and uniqueness.

A Metal Horse does not miss any social gathering where it can show off its charm. They are beautiful, but uncontrollable, and sometimes even daring. They possess a social character, and are very productive, with an incomparable resilience.

Although he lacks stability and patience, he corrects these faults with tolerant thinking. He has sky-high self-esteem and a strong sex appeal. He is seductive, sensitive, and talkative, but at the same time irascible and stubborn.

Water Horse

Water Horses may give up their own interests for those of others. They are susceptible and romantic. They are friendly and it is amazingly comfortable for them to make other people feel firm and satisfied because of their calm personality and affection.

The Water Horse is loquacious, subtle, and interesting. It has ability, mental acuity and always achieves its goals.

Perception and risk-taking make it easy for him to float divinely in difficult contexts, so he always comes out on top in all financial business activities, becoming a shareholder, advisor, or entrepreneur.

Failures, even small ones, deprive you of the ability to think clearly and calmly, limiting you to find an appropriate way out for them and take on another project.

They are super concerned about their health, which is why they are always active, doing physical work, or practicing sports.

He is a Horse with an excellent eye for business, but is very tense about his luck, and comfort. He accommodates easily to new things and tolerates change without blinking. This is a wandering Horse and is more impatient than other Horses.

After deciding, you can change it hundreds of times, in diverse ways, without notifying or explaining it to anyone.

Wooden Horse

Wood Horses possess an exuberant imagination. They are highly respected because of their astute observations of setbacks, and they often know what others are thinking.

They are prone to be fussy, are born as ringleaders, and leave their workers no cause for regret because of their sound and sensible determinations at work.

The Wooden Horse is optimistic. They are respected for their persistence, and profound sense of humor. They are fair, intelligent, and with their conviction, they will guide anyone and prove that they were right. Their principles never compromise them.

Trustworthy in every way, often trusted with secrets, or asked for advice, they are friendly, helpful, and much more patient than other Horses, in fact, they are the most intelligent of all. If you push them, they will be disgruntled.

He is disciplined and able to think clearly and persistently, he is incredibly happy and active. He is not selfish and does not like to abuse others.

It is flamboyant and unsentimental, comfortably eliminates the old and gleefully opens the gate to the new. Firsts always shake his intelligence, and he is not afraid to be unusual.

His duties come first. In an energetic, enlightened, and radiant Horse, but he must be more methodical.

Fire Horse

Fire Horses are magnanimous, full of frenzy, and have the potential to lead the way in art-related business.

Fire Horses have a rigid demeanor and rarely take recommendations from others due to their stubborn personality. Nevertheless, they can face great conflicts, or be under pressure.

The Fire Horse is a cyclone, he is magnificent. A profuse and tenacious actor, his life is full of social gatherings. In his environment, life always burns, but he has enough time and will for anything. This Horse is a preacher, he can rule in any business.

He perceives recommendations with rivalry and as an attempt to keep him out of business. Many admire the Fire Horse for his positive character and sense of humor, but qualities such as rudeness often undermine this opinion.

Impressive and ambitious, the Horse is endowed with brilliant intelligence and personal charisma. He tries to change what he desires with will and restraint. Being daring, he advances towards his goals without caution.

It is a very emotional and irascible temperament. The Fire Horse is comfortable and easy to confuse. It is capricious and hates to perform monotonous tasks.

Earth Horse

Earth Horses are cheerful, reasonable, and willing to help their friends, therefore, they are always surrounded by friends.

They are very responsible and courageous and are often accepted as bosses. They are surrounded by love, although sometimes, due to their spiteful character, they make some mistakes.

The Earth Horse always works hard to achieve success, and this is the reason he usually achieves prosperity throughout his life.

An Earth Horse will reflect more than a thousand times before deciding.

He is not fond of solitude and finds it hard to disconnect from his family. He hates routine, and if by chance this happens in his relationship, his life becomes a hell leading him to suffer serious difficulties. Nevertheless, he is generous and honest. He is a flexible parent and often overlooks his responsibilities.

Their energy is infinite, it is convenient for them to work on their own, as they find it exceedingly difficult to accept orders.

Goats

Metal Goat

Metal Goats are ambitious, slow, and respectful of their values. They are a bit stubborn and have a tough time adapting to the unexpected circumstances that life unexpectedly throws their way. However, sometimes luck is on their side, and they unexpectedly win money in gambling or speculating. Of course, this makes them confident and risky, leading them to lose money, sometimes in substantial amounts.

They should invest in the stock market or in real estate because that is the best way to protect their money in case of tough times.

This Goat is talented in business, she is ambitious and if something does not turn out as she planned, she immediately looks for a solution.

They usually judge her as arrogant, but they are not. What happens is that they know she has nothing to hide and if she has something authentic to show, she does it without complications.

They are not people who beat around the bush, they are direct and if they are interested in someone, they let them know it. Otherwise, they will be detached and dry. They are transparent when it comes to their emotions.

Wooden Goat

Wood Goats are friendly, and tender. They can assess a situation from different angles and make an appropriate decision. They invest a lot of energy when they are in love, and when they speak, they are very sincere and direct, i.e., transparent.

Sometimes they maintain superficial relationships because they are afraid to give free rein to their feelings. They do this because of a lack of security. They are reserved with their private life but are friendly and fun with other people.

They can solve other people's problems with a wisdom that is often lacking in their own personal matters. They are charming, methodical, studious and have a very logical mind.

They can analyze the most complex circumstances. However, they are sometimes so thorough that they delay the execution of difficult ideas. They can see all angles of a situation, so it is difficult for them to reach firm conclusions.

Their interest in excellence leads them to excel. They are good at number-related professions. Logic is their best partner.

Water Goat

Water Goats have a conforming and kind personality. They are receptive to the feelings of others and respond tactfully to the suffering of others. They are loved by those around them because they have a sympathetic, affectionate, and cordial character, and they are not a threat to those who wish to be in positions of authority.

They tend to adapt very easily to circumstances, and do not like to take the initiative to solve any problem. They are more concerned with other people's problems than with their own. Water Goats tend to live more emotionally than rationally, and more reflectively than mentally.

They do not like to feel secluded, and they do not respect conventions. But neither do they have enough energy and motivation to fight against the instituted power. Most of the time they isolate themselves into a world of fantasies in which their potentials can give them benefits.

They possess a lot of artistic talent. They usually sacrifice their time to give service to someone in need, and this makes them very loved in their environment. When they fall in love, they are very faithful and give themselves to that person without thinking about it. With them the saying "till death do us part" is true.

Fire Goats

Fire Goats are enterprising, and they enjoy starting a project or being part of a new idea. Seeing a project grow and reach elevated levels is one of the greatest stimuli this Goat can experience.

Her leadership skills enable her to bring together teams with elevated levels of motivation and alignment with their goals. She is very courageous and aggressive; she stands up for everyone around her. She has no preferences, no matter if they are friends, or work colleagues. Whoever dares to harm a person she esteems or loves, never comes out unscathed.

Fire Goats are amazingly comfortable with risks and deal very well with provocations, they never feel threatened, nor do they give up in a fight. Sometimes, their perseverance is not positive because when they have the tools to succeed, their energy is drained, and they lose vitality.

Some of these Goats are not thrifty and love to party and party, which leads them to make large financial investments because they buy new clothes every time, they have a social gathering.

Earth Goat

The Earth Goat attaches immense importance to traditions and stability. Stubbornness is equally ingrained. They are masters of reason, and it is exceedingly difficult for these Goats to see points of view unless they are the same as their own. They are very demanding people, with great emotional energy.

This Goat is also an optimist, and his desire to succeed combined with his ability to fight, allows him a greater willingness, discipline, and the realization of his most transformative ideals.

In the love sphere, this Earth Goat is endowed with an incomparable ability to understand others, showing sympathy and solidarity with the pain of others. They are attracted to people who are difficult or require extra work to win them over.

Sometimes it alternates between moments of speed and slowness. Sometimes when paralyzed it becomes a destructive force.

Monkeys

Metal Overalls

The Metal Monkey is mischievous, and sometimes falls victim to his own tricks. This Monkey is often teased among his friends.

They are very vain, take diligent care of themselves, and enjoy good physical vitality. They endure heroic efforts and manifest an exceptional potential for work.

On a professional level, their rebelliousness makes them achieve their goals to the end, even if they know they are making a mistake, they do not regret it. These Metal Monkeys are good at manipulating scenarios involving money and speculative transactions because it excites them.

The Metal Monkey, when in love, they are sensual, romantic, and very cordial.

This Monkey possesses an excellent memory. With such a sophisticated memory, they tend to be resentful and remain endlessly imprisoned in this dismal emotion.

She communicates openly, is abrupt, and tactless. Because she does not take herself very seriously, she does not realize how much her jokes can hurt.

Water Monkey

Water Monkeys enjoy being the center of attention and are designed to be leaders. However, they often crush others with their arrogant nature, which is why they are disliked in their close circle.

Water Monkeys are very frugal and reserved, and do not like recommendations from other people. He is a person full of tactics that allow him to start business deals and finish them successfully. He is very distrustful, but extremely helpful, and at every moment he will be trying to heal the relationships that he himself has ruined.

He is persistent, does not believe in the impossible and is skilled at finding the positive side of any difficulty. This Monkey knows how humans work and uses this reasoning to achieve his goals.

You may feel enormous fears, which do not really exist, and without them your path would be more comfortable. Their uncertainty and confused temperament may be the authors of these baseless worries. They overthink things, idealize scenes, and like to anticipate events.

Wooden Monkey

The Wooden Monkey is cheerful, and compassionate. He has an emphasized sense of responsibility and is sometimes a perfectionist. He lacks self-esteem and is an idealist who is fascinated by the new and the modern. Being so impatient, he makes many mistakes and can himself ruin his own projects.

The Wooden Monkey has many genuine friends who always lend a helping hand when he is in trouble, but he does not like to meddle in other people's affairs.

They love any activity that challenges their intellect, keeps them alert and busy, and if it is something fun, all the better. This Wood Monkey loves to be given attention, to be right, and to be thanked for their successes. This can create a conflict because when they do not get what they want they get discouraged easily. In more serious situations they must put a lot of effort into not giving up.

They give much importance to their sexual area, beauty, and attraction. They are meticulous and like their partner to feel happy by their side. Occasionally they are very insistent on their own views and are prone to create conflict in any relationship.

Fire Monkey

The Fire Monkey is always eager for new and different things, they tend to ignore the advantages of traditional things. They always try to combine the new with the traditional. Sometimes they are excessively selfish, which is why people around them get annoyed with them.

They are calculating and opportunistic. They have a head for business and can be involved in several plans at the same time. Their concepts tend to be autonomous and far from archetypes.

The Fire Monkey is admired at work for his gifted mind. They are very energetic, self-confident, and determined. They are intuitive in relation to the collective subconscious and possess excellent organizational skills.

The Fire Monkey is the strongest of all the Monkeys, likes to control, and as a result, they are sought after for the good judgment they make regarding various things. The Fire Monkey is always open to innovative ideas, and in times of stress shows their stubborn side. When this stubbornness hits them, they become inflexible and try to impose their opinions on others.

Ground Monkey

The Earth Monkey is optimistic and bold, is very polite and respects his values, and those of others. They are very patient and calmly and confidently accomplish their goals.

These Monkeys are not spenders, but they are not selfish either, on the contrary, they love to do charitable works that earn them the respect of society.

They love freedom and give others the same freedom they desire. However, they take great care of their family and friends. They sporadically appear eccentric, their thoughts are difficult, and they find it difficult to reveal their emotions to others.

The Earth Monkey does not like to entertain others but is sincerely kind to those they care about and love. They have a propensity to be tense people because they have a tough time relaxing, specifically when it comes to matters related to their family.

Earth Monkeys if they expose their negative side are insecure, but their determination and focus override that quality. In general, they care about the impression they make.

Roosters

Metal Rooster

The Metal Rooster has a shrewd and critical mind. They possess a courage that is enviable, which enables them to face any crisis with determination and bravery. This Rooster is noticeably clear in his mind about what is important to him. He never deviates from his purposes and goals.

The Metal Rooster likes to be flattered because he strives for his qualities to be seen by others. He is an excellent negotiator, and his practicality captivates more than one person.

Under the influence of Metal, this Rooster is enraptured with the idea of being important and famous, fights tirelessly for it and his pride does not allow him to put aside this goal. To obtain this purpose, if necessary, they can give up things that they like, or give pleasure, throwing themselves with their eyes closed and not allowing anything, or anyone, to stand in the way of their ascent.

The Metal Rooster possesses excellent social skills and is not interested in resisting provocations and obstacles that come his way.

Water Rooster

Water Roosters always have a card up their sleeve, and the ability to face and resolve any conflict or problem that comes their way. They are modest and compassionate with everyone who crosses their path, they show love when they have the opportunity and are super diligent workers.

The Water Rooster is polite, elegant, and persistent and will always fight to the end to achieve his goals. He is admired for these qualities, plus he adds to them a unique and true sense of humor.

This Rooster thinks clearly and practically. He does not like to criticize or judge others. He can be a great writer or a preacher with the power to lead masses of people and push them to act. His Achilles heel is that sometimes he becomes a robot and stops seeing the trees to look at the forest.

The Water Rooster knows that life can be lived with joy, and for this he feels gratitude. He demonstrates this with a twinkle in his eye and a unique and exclusive confidence.

When it is unavoidable, they feel pessimism, but they have limits because they perceive that everything can get better soon.

Wooden Rooster

Wood Roosters are very sociable, humorous and love their family above all things. They are very trusting, and this sometimes works against them as bad people take advantage of this.

This Rooster is incredibly lucky for money, he can go to bed without a penny and the next day a business appears where he earns thousands of dollars. In general, success is their ally, even in tough times. They have a kind but restless character and are active people who do not like to feel restricted. They care about innovative ideas, or places where they can get a lot of knowledge.

The Wooden Rooster is very sociable, open-minded, and because he is not so stubborn, his life is extremely easy.

One of the most distinctive characteristics of these Roosters is their willingness to keep humor present in every minute, hour, and day of their lives. They can joke about their shortcomings, and when they are feeling down, they can usually find amusement in life and have fun with what they possess at the time. They are labeled as naïve, but really, they often have their own description of what wellness is.

Fire Rooster

The Fire Rooster places a value on loyalty that is unmatched by anything else. They have honor and what they promise they deliver. Their values are non-negotiable, and for that reason they are leaders wherever they are.

A detective par excellence, he can gather information in the blink of an eye and draw accurate conclusions. He can be stubborn and loves to put everything and everyone under a magnifying glass for analysis.

Because they naturally know how to negotiate, they are great when you entrust them with the mission of looking out for your interests, as they are super resourceful in aligning financial issues. Their opinions are engaging, interesting and inspiring. They are prone to be very sincere and are quite direct when they must tell you a truth.

They tend to consider the moments of metamorphosis as incredibly significant resources to have a greater lucidity in relation to their deepest fears during their life.

Ground Rooster

Ground Roosters are very enthusiastic and generous. Travel is their favorite pastime, and their prestige is something they defend to the hilt. They analyze everything as if they were scientists and create their own data base and then act without making mistakes. They do not get distracted in the process and eliminate from their path anything that smells like a distraction from their objectives.

His example is worth following, and although he leads a simple life, his work is remarkable.

When they are with someone, they have a habit of reading between the lines of the relationship, they want to know everything, and they have a compelling need to control their environment or create techniques for that. They are not impatient and tend to plan their initial moves in a careful and curious manner, believing in their potential to read others and the circumstances around them.

While they can be a little tenacious, they are determined, and will fight to the end to get what they want, even if it means tirelessly engaging in altercations.

Dog

Metal Dog

The Metal Dog is elegant and sexy. This Dog always has many suitors around him because of his beauty. When they are looking for a love relationship, they want someone stable, for that reason they always look for a person who does not live on illusions.

They are enthusiastic, but if they become disillusioned it is exceedingly difficult to regain their confidence and passion. They seek commitment and stability and lack patience with fickle people. They are attracted to people who are down to earth, and trusting their partners is especially important to them. They must learn to manage their need to control, because that is the only way to overcome their possessiveness.

Their most prized virtue is patience; everything they start they finish. They have a supernatural strength of mind that makes them persevere, prudent, and thoughtful.

The Metal Dog knows that getting angry is the resort of fools, but when they get irritated it is difficult to dominate them, especially in matters related to their partner.

Water Dog

The Water Dog has a master's degree in planning, is courageous and resents being traditional. However, he loves his family and all those he considers to be people who deserve his attention. He is sensitive to the needs of those in need and is always willing to go the extra mile to help them.

He is exceedingly kind to himself and to others, sometimes he is capricious, but he knows how to control his emotions. He is a good friend and counselor. He does not live by illusions and is extremely strict because he desires positive relationships. When he manages to balance external perception and intuition, he reasons correctly.

Despite their excellent intellectual capacity and charisma, they do not aspire to leadership positions because of their concern for equality. For them it is important to achieve a cordial relationship, and sometimes they prefer to accept circumstances that make them suffer for fear of being left alone.

Although they do not tolerate injustice, they consider the opinion of others and do not like to be criticized or judged. They are super accommodating and sympathetic in their relationships because their purpose is to be accepted and loved.

Wooden Dog

Wood Dogs are respected and communicate politely with others.

They are good economists since they know how to incorporate the gloomy
and to seek balance. Your success is related to that of your company or family. Accumulate resources by will and constancy, on behalf of your family.

His energy is sometimes annoying because he has a strong will that overthrows any obstacle. When he shows his positive side, he is rebellious, determined, and sensible. If he exposes his dark side, he can be distrustful, resentful, and irritable.
This Dog is excessively sensual, but a terrifying enemy, capable of violent hatred when annoyed. They cannot be fooled, because they find out everything, and if there is a disloyalty it will mean a giant effort to turn the page.

As a father he tends to be demanding and strict. But because of his ability to enjoy life, he is a friend of his children.

Sometimes they receive bequests, or family assets, which they end up hiding.

Fire Dog

The Fire Dog is intelligent and hardworking. They always get all their work done on time, but they disperse their energy too much because of their lack of focus. They are very influenced by other people and by the environment.

A Fire Dog is honest and has a high willingness to help those in need. Their calm, yet cheerful temperament makes them the life and soul of any social gathering. They sometimes lose their sense of tact, and their desire to find the truth leads them to express their opinions, regardless of who they affect. The fire that rules this sign is not diplomatic, but it is inspiring.

It has incredible seductive power but is challenging when it rebels. They prefer steady, continuous earnings. They know how difficult it is for them to earn the money they need, something that is compounded by their lack of foresight in this area.

They have good mental concentration, and the ability to become totally immersed in their work. Seems to know things on an instinctive, non-verbal level, and prefers to learn through direct experience or apprenticeship, rather than through books or lectures.

He has mechanical skill in his hands. He can become very skilled at pottery, carpentry, or anything else that involves manual labor. He has conflicting emotional needs that complicate his personal life. He has a keen sense of purpose and instinctively knows that, to achieve anything admirable, he must eliminate the redundant, and devote himself totally to the purpose he wishes to achieve.

Earth Dog

The Earth Dog is calm, affectionate, and reserved. His performance depends on the firmness between what he says and what he does. That is the reason it is preferable for him to think first what he says Rather than to rectify what he said, or to simulate what was done.

This Dog can become a person of authority or power in the intellectual world. He has a lightning intuition that comes out at specific times in a quite accurate way. Their challenge is to lower their level of emotional tension, so that their true intuition emerges. Otherwise, your affective behaviors will be detached, cold, and prone to ill-considered breakups.

This Dog needs to combine affection with freedom, which is difficult, but attainable. The keys to achieving this are respect for other people, and brotherly communication.

You often get nervous about other people's emotional reactions, which you see as alien to your own nature. It would be advisable for you to find out empirically about human psychology to be more tolerant of the different emotional forces of the people around you.

Pig

Metal Pig

Metal Pigs are friendly, and value loyalty highly. They are efficient and bold. They are noted for their sense of humor. They are extroverted and show their affection openly. They possess vision, enterprising ideas, and an instinct for gambling, all of which contribute to their success in the business world. However, his confidence can also cause him problems because he sometimes promises more than he can deliver, misses significant details to be criticized, and may overestimate the potential of an idea.

The Metal Pig possesses excellent powers of concentration and enjoys studying or deep thought in solitude. They are level-headed and Rational, with the ability to get to the heart of any argument and can quickly see weaknesses in other people's logic.

This Pig enjoys working on problems that others consider too boring, and technical. They tend to devote themselves to some area of knowledge and become engrossed in all the details of that area, sometimes ignoring that few people share their personal interest, especially at their level.

He has ties to his past, the place where he was born, and family traditions. It is not possible for him to break with the habits and roles learned during his childhood. The connection with his mother is strong, and this Pig seeks affection and protection from his partner and other members of his family.

Water Pig

Water Pigs do not express themselves easily, even when they have a lot to say. His mind tends to wander, and he finds it difficult to study very realistic subjects that do not have much color or idealism. His perception and the first emotions he feels are likely to be accurate, with a tendency to rely on this ability to make decisions. He has an expressive predisposition, and the faculty to reach out to others in a friendly way.

His emotional greatness, and lack of pettiness is much admired in his circle of friends, and they often look to him for help or advice. He is always ready to overlook the faults of others and sometimes goes overboard with compassion.

He has an inner attitude and balance that allows him to proceed efficiently during trauma and emotional stress. He maintains objectivity around emotionally charged issues, often to the distress of others who would like him to react more forcefully.

This Pig experiences strong attractions of great emotional and sexual potency and may feel that he has little control over his desires. They have a pervasive need for love and can be emotionally insatiable. His love life is enthusiastic, turbulent, and painful. Jealousy, power struggles, and manipulation can become areas of conflict in their relationships.

He faces many challenges, and many obstacles in pursuing his purposes and desires. These setbacks often occur because this Pig has done things in haste or tried to work according to his will without regard for the impact on others.

Wooden Pig

Wood Pigs take their goals seriously and know that keeping working is the only way to achieve them. Persistent effort, and concentration on a single objective are the ways he achieves his goals in life.

He stoically faces difficulties and will patiently struggle through problems. He knows deep down inside that he can only depend on himself, that everything is on his back, and he can be very inflexible in instilling discipline, as he has lofty expectations.

This Pig often limits himself, doubting his own ability. He feels he meets great resistance when he tries to be assertive, and this can be very frustrating. However, he can be consistent, and the determination to overcome all obstacles.

Politeness, good manners, and proper behavior are especially important to this Pig. His calm, objective attitude is, to others, primarily, and while he is indeed extremely helpful, he does not radiate much sympathy, so others may not see that side of his temperament immediately.

He may appear methodical and objective and even more conservative than he is at heart. He is the type of person to go to for advice, or to ask for an unbiased opinion, but not for emotional support.

The Wood Pig is very practical and wants to see tangible results of her efforts, as she is not one to weave crazy dreams. All her dreams have to do with material achievements, and security, as she has a great love for the physical world and wants to enjoy it to the fullest.

Fire Pig

The Fire Pig has three main defects, one of which is his stubborn stubbornness. The second is his lack of interest in deviating from his comfortable routine, and the third is his tendency to devalue the imaginative, the speculative and the fanciful, in other words, the inability to play with ideas and possibilities, and to open his mind to the new.

When the Fire Pig decides what he wants to do, he does it with tenacity, and if necessary, he will sacrifice himself to achieve his deep convictions. This trait is not common, and, in fact, tends to make him feel a bit out of place in relation to others.

He takes things very formally and tends to be a bit of a fanatic, though probably not overtly so, so others may not know how much he is affected and driven by things that are important. He has a resolute will and a willingness to strive to achieve things that have real meaning, rather than following an easier, but less meaningful course in life.

He doubts his intelligence and mental abilities and works extremely hard with his studies to remedy this. He is often profoundly serious and disinterested in small talk, and general conversations are difficult for him.

Ground Hog

Earth Pigs cannot tolerate pettiness of any kind and tend to exaggerate. They also have a beautiful sense of drama. The desire for personal recognition, and the need to do something they are proud of, motivate them strongly. They have an unusual capacity for fun and mischief.

He is entrepreneurial and has a keen interest in making it big. He is always on the lookout for new opportunities and business ventures and is willing to take risks if he senses that he is after a win. No matter what he achieves, he never is completely satisfied. He always feels he can do more and sets his sights on another goal.

He feels frustrated in limited circumstances and would abandon scenarios of relative success and security if they do not offer him the potential to expand and grow in the future. He likes to keep pushing his limits, to see how far he can go.

This Pig tends to lose patience very easily, especially with indecisive people. They need to see immediate results, and cannot stand to wait, which can lead them to rush their decisions. They need to learn to think before speaking or acting, because many times they will act on impulse, complicating the situation or exposing themselves to dangerous situations.

Ritual to start the Chinese New Year 2024

The Chinese New Year should be welcomed with joy, music, and a splendid family meal. It is a period to celebrate and concentrate on luck and prosperity for the coming year. You should wear new clothes because this symbolizes a new beginning. A resonant color, such as red, which represents harmony, good luck, and well-being, is great for this day. Avoid wearing white or black while waiting for the New Year, as these are the colors people usually wear for funerals.

Doing a cleaning to be prepared for the Chinese New Year, in the form of a ritual, is beneficial. This cleaning is intended to ward off evil spirits that may be hiding in the corners of the house. Usually, people change the furniture or move it, touch up the paint in their home, repair what is damaged, and wash the windows with abundant water.

Purification Ritual

That same evening, before the beginning of the year, you should clean your house, open all the windows for ventilation, and place white and red flowers in all the communal areas of your home. Specifically at the entrance you should place cinnamon, sandalwood, eucalyptus, or lavender incense, or burn laurel leaves. Laurel is a plant that can protect, purify, and heal. Another way to attract positive energies to your home is by combining cinnamon with bay leaves. Burn bay leaves and sprinkle cinnamon powder over them. When this mixture is lit, spread the smoke throughout the rooms of your house.

You must smoke the house well. To smoke is the action of creating smoke, using incense, to aromatize the environment, and to use it as an instrument of purification and cleaning. Its particularity is that they expel a pleasant fragrance, to which relaxing properties are attributed. Many people use incense burners to change the energetic vibrations of their home.

If you have an incense that you are going to pass throughout the house, remember to make circular movements to the right. If you intend to purify a personal area, you should begin with your own body starting from your feet up to your head, and then return to the heart, always making light circles.

As this is the year of the Green Wooden Dragon it is advisable to have a pair of wooden Dragons in your home. If you do not have that opportunity, you can symbolize it with images, portraits, or figures.

Another recommendation for the year 2024 is to paint some of the walls of your house green. This color symbolizes prosperity for this year. Do not saturate your house with green, remember to maintain balance. If you overdo it with green, you will attract stress to your life.

Another alternative or option is to carry it with you, as a bracelet, pendant earrings, pendulums, sleepers, on a ring, keychain or talisman in your pocket or purse, this will form an association of wealth, shelter and good luck in your life, home, or office.

If you can buy some plants such as Lavender, Rue, or the money plant, which have the capacity to generate abundance, in addition to their power to move away and transmute bad vibrations, you will not regret it.

As water is the element that complements wood, a water fountain at the entrance of your home will attract prosperity. Do not forget that water should flow inward. Placing a water fountain in the wealth area of your home, located on the left side, at the back, looking from the front door, will bring you many material gains.

Along with green, red is the lucky color for this year 2024, you should use it in your home to activate the energies of good luck. You can wear red on your clothes, or with some other garment such as a scarf, a cap, or a bracelet so you can attract money.

Predictions for 2024

Rat

This year 2024, the Rat will have particularly good prospects in his profession because he can generate profits. If you have a stable job, you will generate good income and will have the opportunity for a salary increase. If you are offered the opportunity to change your job, you should think about it before deciding. Observe and analyze before making any move. If your intuition tells you that the new job will help you achieve your career goals, accept the challenge.

The Rat has a good chance of advancement in the year 2024, as Dragon years always offer many financial and professional opportunities. Since Rats are so resourceful, they will be able to earn extra money, and establish contacts with influential people. Business travel and study can pay off for this hardworking sign.

For self-employed Rats or entrepreneurs, hard work and strategic ideas can pay off, helping them advance their businesses.

The Year of the Dragon is about expanding networks and making valuable connections. Rats can connect with influential people and form beneficial partnerships that will open doors to new opportunities.

They should be incredibly careful with the insincerity of work colleagues, if they get into disputes or legal problems, you may lose a lawsuit.

It is best to avoid conflicts to avoid unpleasant surprises.

There will be periods where you will earn a lot of money, however, you should be careful with impulsive spending and not invest without studying the market.

Wood Dragon energies are extraordinarily strong and can bring challenges. Rats may experience increased stress, so it is important to stay balanced. Rats will experience a personal transformation during 2024, which will bring them to a deeper understanding of their life's purpose.

The prospects will be favorable in love, you have many opportunities to interact and establish new relationships. Within your work circle, if you are single, there is the possibility of finding your soul mate.

Rats will be able to enjoy a stable love life, whether they have a steady partner or not. Those who are already engaged may decide to expand their family.

You should pay attention to your kidneys and urinary system. Finding the time to exercise is fundamental, more outdoor activities, walking, jogging, or cycling are good options. You should take advantage of sunlight to improve your health. The most important source of vitamin D comes from sun exposure. You should expose your face and hands to the sun for 5 to 10 minutes daily so that you can increase the vitamin D in your body.

Ox

During the Year of the Dragon, the Ox will feel full of energies, but they should be overly cautious because this year brings very profound changes, positive impacts, but also some challenging ones.

The Ox is a highly ethical and determined individual, these qualities will intensify and provide the Ox with an extra measure of perseverance. They will be willing to face any challenge and pursue their goals with an indestructible will.

This year of the Dragon will present the Ox with many opportunities for professional success. They will get recognition in their professional endeavors, their willingness, tolerance, and level of commitment will finally be rewarded.

The creation of a network of contacts can help them in their professional development, and even if their work responsibilities increase, they will be able to move forward with enthusiasm. The Dragon's energy will guide the Ox and give him strategies to become more prosperous, but he needs to invest and manage his finances. Although the Ox is financially responsible, and the year of the Dragon will give him opportunities for prosperity, it is crucial that he learns to manage his finances and avoid unnecessary risks.

The Ox should remember that all challenges are for the purpose of evaluating your patience and ability to adapt; these challenges are opportunities for personal growth and development. It is not that the Dragon is going to put money directly into your hands. It is that you will find investment opportunities and if you make the right choices, you will achieve prosperity.

If you do not have a partner, you must be patient, there are opportunities, but you will also find competition. Your chance to find love may be hidden within your group of friends.

The funny thing is that you will be more likely to find a partner if you are not looking that hard. You are likely to meet someone casually Rather than in an actual romantic setting.

If you are currently in a relationship, you must prevent love from falling into a routine, for that you will have to make efforts and have a lot of tolerance and patience. The stress of work and family conflicts can provoke arguments that can alienate you from your partner. Communication is especially important, and maturity is fundamental.

In the event of a dispute or litigation, both parties will suffer substantial losses. The smart thing to do is to seek a reconciliation with the other party so that you can avoid significant monetary loss.

During the Year of the Dragon, you will have good health and energy. They will only suffer from insomnia due to stress, so it would be advisable to find a way to relax.

If you are more in touch with your emotions this can help you evolve this year. Exercise when you can and be sure to watch your diet. If you maintain healthy eating habits, you will have a decent year.

Tiger

The year of the Wood Dragon will bring obstacles to the Tiger's professional area. It is especially important that when you encounter these difficulties, you do not make any mistakes. You must remain calm and use your wisdom.

You should not get involved in any discussions with your work colleagues, or clients, to avoid any adverse impact. Tigers are popular for their confident nature, this quality will intensify, and they will be inclined to take risks. They can be successful if they maintain their competitive spirit and establish new contacts or influential connections during this year.

Those who have a stable job will experience some difficult months and will need patience to deal with their bosses.

Tigers possess a strong financial sense, and the year of the Dragon may present them with opportunities to increase their finances. However, they should manage their finances wisely, take advantage of appropriate opportunities and avoid impulsive spending.

The Year of the Dragon is always promising, but it can bring challenges, which will evaluate the Tigers' capacity for adaptability. It is a year to explore new horizons. You should concentrate on your responsibilities, it is not a time to scatter your energies or be distracted by useless matters, it is a time to accumulate experiences.

You will enjoy good relationships with those around you, those in the initial stages of a romance or starting one during the Wooden Dragon year should allow the relationship to develop in its own time. Being rushed or having expectations in the initial stages could lead to shipwreck.

For those of you with a partner, the year can be busy and interesting. Not only will there be plans and hopes to share, but as situations change, there will also be new opportunities. You need to be communicative and talk things over with your partner and share and make joint efforts. Your charisma will be irresistible, but if you are in a relationship, focus on deepening emotional connections.

You must talk seriously with people who have caused you problems in your life because, although it is a year to strengthen friendships, you must get rid of those who do not contribute anything positive to your life.

Tigers are advised to manage stress and exercise daily to maintain physical and mental health. Meditation can help them improve their overall well-being. You should quit smoking and strengthen your mind.

Prevention is better than cure, so, in case of any illness, consult a specialist immediately. Pay attention to your energy levels. A balanced diet and regular exercise will contribute to your overall well-being. Participate in activities that stimulate your mind. Practice mindfulness to relieve stress. Make sure you balance work and rest to maintain optimal health.

Rabbit

During the Year of the Dragon, Rabbits will develop an extraordinary sense of creativity. They will be inclined to explore their artistic talents and will have opportunities for professional development.

Work will be the place of refuge for the Rabbits, and those who have a job will be successful as they may receive a salary increase or a change to a more senior position.

Those who do not have a job will be able to get that job of which they have always dreamed. It is important not to get carried away by impatience. This is the ideal time to focus on your physical fitness and mental well-being, channeling your energies into creative activities.

Rabbits possess a keen sense of fiscal management. The year of the Dragon comes for you with many opportunities to prosper financially.

This will be a variable year, those who have a partner should be careful with infidelities. It is important not to get carried away by friends, some may give you bad advice.

Those who do not have a partner should be careful if they are looking for one, because the year will bring many opportunities that can be a trap that can make them suffer. Your charismatic personality will be a magnet for all relationships.

If you are already in a romantic relationship, be prepared to make it even better than it has been in recent years. Pay attention to your partner to enhance the intimacy of your sexual relationship.

Tigers may encounter conflict when interacting with others. In the event of an argument, if it is a legitimate and reasonable cause, you will win. With the Dragon backing you up, you can achieve an overwhelming victory.

You should pay attention to your digestive system; you should follow a more varied diet. Your body is your sacred temple. There is no point in taking care of all the other aspects of your life if your body is neglected.

This year you may miss someone who left your life, life is like that, it gives you good things that you should enjoy now, and it also takes them away when you least expect it. You must continue generating beautiful memories, memories that make you feel, in the end it is the only thing we will take with us.

In some months of the year, you will be dealing with wounds you thought were closed.

The family environment will be pleasant, you will be able to buy a house or rent a place to live.

By the end of the year, work will become more stressful. That means you will have to work harder and work with other people more often. Colleagues at work may seem more annoying than usual. However, try to remain calm when dealing with them.

Dragon

This year the Dragon will have a stable and prosperous career, which will allow you not only professional success but also economic prosperity. If there is a job with promotion possibilities, it will be yours. It does not mean that you will not meet competitors, but you will conquer that position because you will be able to demonstrate your true abilities.

You will also be able to make investments in real estate, education, and other ventures, and although the progress of the investments may be slow, you will eventually make a profit.

A relationship with a partner may deteriorate, but despite that you will advance in your business. At the beginning of the year, you may have some quarrel with your partner, or you may lack mutual understanding on some work matter, as the year progresses, you will eliminate that misunderstanding and make decisions in the interest of business.

In their quest for prestige, Dragons may encounter people with whom they disagree, which will lead to some fights, the best approach is to solve the problem as quickly as possible. Avoid mental and physical exhaustion and waste of time.

This year, if you manage to bring out your more diplomatic and mature side, 2024 promises a lot for you, especially for Dragons who have a steady partner or are looking for stability. By overcoming the challenges that stand in your way, you will feel closer than ever to your partner.

Singles will meet a kindred spirit and the two will be able to establish a lasting relationship.

You should pay attention to your throat, lungs, and respiratory system in general. It is recommended that you avoid polluted air.

Too much stress can cause muscle aches and reluctance to engage in physical activity, which can be detrimental to your health. A healthy and balanced diet, drinking water, eliminating coffee and alcohol will help you maintain your ideal weight. Sport would help you to maintain your emotional and physical balance.

2024 will be a year of success if you do not trust everyone. If you work hard at your job and take care of financial details, your professional status and reputation will rise. There is a possibility of some travel related to your work, and even if you do not like to wait, this year you should be patient and cautious to sow with intelligence and calmness. If you manage to do so, you can reap great successes and profits in the future.

You will have to work hard to communicate with your family, especially with your children. You will not agree with the way they act or the decisions they make. You will be misunderstood.

Snake

Get ready for 2024, because your charisma will increase, and you will become the soul of every meeting. You will attract people without the slightest effort. Everyone will invite you and want to be with you. You will know how to move with influential people, and this year your ambition will be rewarded. Be careful who you talk to, what kind of people you relate to, or you will make mistakes. You will meet new people, who will open the doors of new environments and businesses, but once again, the advice is not to be hasty and analyze well with whom you associate if you do not want to fall into the nets of a predator. It will be a fabulous year for you.

Good year for love. If you have a partner, you will be happy, but you will analyze your relationship discreetly. You will see clearly what you must change to be fully happy. You will be sure whether you should continue or break up. If you are single, your intention is to conquer everyone you can. You are willing to seduce, to fall in love and to have fun. There is no one who can stop your passion.

Some could find the right person and live a precious enthusiastic love. If you have a boyfriend/girlfriend, this will be a definitive year in your relationship, since you could realize that this is the person of your life and decide to get engaged or even married, or you could realize that he/she is not the right person for you and decide to break up. If so, break up as soon as possible and turn the page and throw the book away. If you do not, you will be trapped in a toxic and unhappy relationship that will get you nowhere.

You like money very much, you know how to earn it, but it gets out of your hands easily. This year, powerful energies will move, and you will have to learn to retain it, reflect and think well how to spend it or invest it, before making any kind of movement, otherwise you will lose your economic stability. Do not contract debts, if you already have them pay them, you should invest in the real estate sector. Be careful with your expenses and you will do well.

Many opportunities will come your way this year, but you should consult with your family before making decisions. You could buy your own house or have a child.

If you take care of yourself, your health will be good. Do not overindulge in food, drinks and respect the hours of sleep. Take care of your body, your digestive system and especially your intestines. With proper nutrition, everything will be fine.

If you feel discomfort in your eyesight, or difficulty focusing your vision, go to the Ophthalmologist for a diagnosis. If you do not treat it quickly, you could have severe headaches, which will prevent you from working normally.

During the year of the Wood Dragon, they must make themselves respected, show themselves honorable and beware of intrigues that may involve them. The Snake has a deep knowledge of human nature, and they will see people with bad intentions coming and will know how to deal with them.

Horse

Although 2024 will be a year in which you will need to be careful, you will have opportunities to succeed and achieve your goals. You will suffer some disappointments or be involved in misunderstandings that can make you look bad and put you in unnecessary trouble. Be always cautious with your friendships as some may betray you.

Different points of view and controversies will arise in your home, it is best to clear it up quickly. You will make some good trips with your loved ones. These changes of environment will be good for you as they will allow you to rest, have fun and focus on your life.

It is advisable not to be enthusiastic about any business you have underway because there could be hidden problems that will surprise you. The year will be full of obstacles, but if you solve them as they appear, you will move forward with your initial plans.

Your love life, if you have a partner, will demand a lot of dedication and patience. If you do not have a partner and a new love appears, take the time to get to know this person deeply before making serious decisions. Do not have false illusions or you will suffer a great disappointment.

To acquire new knowledge and improve, you should set aside time for your intellectual growth. You will have a lot of work and challenges to face, and you will have to face new responsibilities, but by trying you will demonstrate your great capacity, knowledge, and professional solidity. The result will be that, although it will be a year of challenging work, you will face it with determination, and you will earn the admirations of others.

You must take care of your economy since you will have unforeseen expenses, try to save, and have a budget if you do not want to have problems with your monthly payments.

Excellent job opportunities will arise, but it will be a close fight between you and your colleagues. Remember that you are a fighter, do not let yourself be intimidated.

Your health will be fantastic and if you practice meditation and everything related to spiritual matters, you will feel great, alive, and dynamic, calm, and balanced. Your image will change, and you will feel extremely attractive. If you can follow a healthy and balanced diet, with fruits and vegetables, you will have an iron health. It all depends on your willpower.

With your children it will be exceedingly difficult for you to find the limit between authority and discipline, you must impose respect in a positive way. If you are thinking of becoming a father or mother during 2024, it is better that you give up this idea, next year you will do much better and everything will flow easily.

Goat

You are a very sociable person, and you are going to have an incredibly fun year 2024, accompanied by your family and best friends, but you will also go through relaxed and quiet periods, in which you will isolate yourself to be with yourself.

You will receive invitations of all kinds, to join groups, it is essential that you learn to say no, and if you want to reduce expenses at home, you must reduce meals, parties, and dinners at restaurants. There you have an escape from a lot of money.

In love, 2024 will be a difficult year. If you are in couple, the relationship will be prone to instability. You will go through good and bad months. You have been too much time focused on your problems and your partner may have felt sad and abandoned. You should clarify this situation in a very sincere conversation. Feelings must be restored. All is not lost, but things are going to be difficult.

If you are single, you will be extremely attractive and magnetic. You could have sporadic partners, but what would make you happy is to find your soul mate. This is not the best time for you to commit yourself. Be careful with people who may approach you out of interest.

At work it will be a little complicated. You must be discreet, to avoid confrontations with your bosses, avoid any conflict. You will have to fight to keep what you have obtained so far. If you are looking for a job, look in several places at the same time so that you can choose comfortably.

If you want to have your own business, do not trust blindly in your partners, get good advice, make a market study, and check all the papers with a lawyer.

During the year 2024 you should be thriftier and more prudent, so as not to go bankrupt. Do not spend unnecessarily, because if the economic instability makes you so nervous you should avoid it by being panic-stricken.

You will be lucky in games of chance this year, do not forget to play because luck may visit you.

Your health will be a little weak, but it will be because of stress. You will be anxious, and this will affect your health. You could have stomach aches by somatizing your nervous states. The best thing to do is to get help from a psychologist.

In 2024 you will be incredibly involved in your home affairs and family problems. Be concerned, but do not be anxious. Learn to see problems with perspective, everything has a solution, and you will manage to fix it. In addition, you will have family projects, trips, and activities in common.

Monkey

This will be an excellent year of positive changes. The Wood Dragon favors you and will push you towards professional and personal success. Money will come into your hands easily and you will be able to make great investments. Be careful, you must be careful because you will be surrounded by people who envy you, and you could even be betrayed.

In 2024 your social life will be continually active and thanks to your professional success you will become the center of attention of your circle of friends and colleagues.

In love you will do very well, thanks to your magnetism and professional success, you will become the center of attention of all eyes and comments. If you are in couple, it will be a stable year, full of happiness. Together you will enjoy your success. If you are single, it could be the year of your engagement.

All the changes that will occur in your area of love are positive, and if you are alone you are guaranteed to find a partner, you will meet many new people and among them will be that great love.

This will be a changing, surprising year. The strength of the Wood Dragon will push you to face changes with self-confidence and courage. If you are looking for work, you will find the job you are looking for. If you already have a job and even if you are not looking to change jobs, you will find several offers that are worth analyzing carefully.

Be incredibly careful with your colleagues because they will be envious of your luck and could complicate your life. This year they could promote you, recognize your worth or raise your salary.

You will live a prosperous year economically, it is the year of your professional recognition, you will enjoy the acquisitive and social level of which you have dreamed. This year, you will be able to save, and it is also the year when you will be able to buy the house of your dreams. Analyze well the real estate market before deciding and the conditions of the house they are selling you.

You will have a year with good health and lots of energy. Your physical strength will accompany you throughout the year. You will have no illnesses and if you catch something, it will be a passing cold. Nothing to worry about. Exercise is advisable, and a healthy and balanced diet is the key to your excellent health.

Within your home there will be peace and harmony. You will share your successes with your family, and they will support you 100%. If you are thinking of having a child, this is the perfect year, one more blessing that will fill this year 2024 with happiness.

Rooster

You will experience great transformations in your life, it will be a year in which you will feel under a lot of pressure and with the need to make important decisions that will give your future clarity and security. You will have moments of uncertainty, but you will take the plunge to feel stabilized. Everything can happen in your life, from moving, breaking up with your partner to job changes.

Love will go well if you have a partner, because your partner will help you to stabilize and reassure you. It will be a convulsive year, but stable in love. The advice is to be affectionate and communicative, but in case of disagreements you should neutralize them immediately. If you are single, it will be exceedingly difficult for you to find a partner. You may fall in love with the wrong person and that would be an extra problem in your life.

Your social life will be active, but you will try to commit less excesses, you will choose your friends better, and exchanges of ideas and meetings will replace the big parties. A pleasant dinner will be more rewarding than a discotheque.

You will have a lot of work and that will make you anxious. If you need to rethink your work life, do it as soon as possible. You will change your profession, because you will be willing to transform your work life if it means recovering your peace of mind. It would be a clever idea for you to take a course to improve your chances in your profession.

In this year 202a you will seek to earn money at all costs, and for that it will be necessary for you to change jobs, to have two jobs or to have your own business. You will be willing to do anything to maintain your economic level. You will have to try, but you will not hesitate to act.

You will become more demanding of yourself, but you will not mind, you will do so to have more money and live the life you want with purchasing power and the ability to travel. These changes will make you a thriftier and more analytical person. You will reduce your expenses and you will have money for vacations.

Your health will be changeable and even if you do not have any disease, you should take care of yourself so as not to fall into depressive states.

You should exercise and practice relaxation techniques. It is important to control your nerves and keep yourself in peace and harmony. Your family will support you and try to calm you down. They will see you extremely nervous and will try to help you find solutions. They can live modestly, but you will not allow that. You will always try to give the best to your family.

Dog

The year 2024 will be an incredibly positive year. Everything will move fast. Many opportunities will arise and the goals that you did not achieve last year, with effort you will be able to achieve them in 2024. At work you will use all your accumulated experience, which will be useful to you this new year. When opportunities arise, you will be placed in the front line, benefiting in every way.

They should be more involved in their workplace or studies; it will also benefit them if they have more initiative and become indispensable.

For those who are looking for a job, if they do their research perfectly, they will find the opportunities they are looking for and will be able to apply without any problems. They should find out which sector would be the most suitable. If they decide to develop a personal project, they will be phenomenally successful. They should find the time to do it, because it will be beneficial and you will have a lot of success, as well as economic gains.

They will have a lot of social life and will enjoy doing activities and getaways with friends. There are travel opportunities.

You will do well in love. If you are single, you will have opportunities to meet special people, fall in love and live a love story. For those who already have a partner, it will be a year to share.

You will transmit your enthusiasm to your family, harmony will reign at home, you will have reasons to Celebrate, and you will feel happy.

Do not waste your energies because you will need them during the year. Do not try to do a thousand things at once, plan and you will have time and energy for everything.

This year they have all the potential to shine and face any challenge, but they must be incredibly careful because it could also be disastrous. They will err on the side of benevolence, want to overextend themselves and play with luck. That said, it can be a successful year if they do things right.

You will carry your responsibilities perfectly, and you will be able to develop your full potential. Keep your lifestyle balanced. Do not be rude to others. Haste and risk are negative.

If you are interested in expanding your knowledge and learning new subjects, 2024 is a good year to study. It is also a year to gain experience and put into practice everything you have learned.

They should exercise, expend energy, and find balance. Beware of doing crazy things because it is a year in which you could get injured.

Pig

This year you will have to use your intuition to adapt to this year's changes. You will have to go beyond your usual efforts to improve yourself. You must use your knowledge and experiences to succeed, and it will be a year where you will be able to excel and study. You will have to make changes in your life and in your way of thinking, otherwise you will fail.

It will be an excellent year for opportunities, which should not be missed. You will have to be always determined and take the plunge. You will be able to prove your worth and go for your goals. Your hobbies and the subjects that interest you could take you further than a simple distraction. They could broaden their knowledge, delving into unknown and especially useful subjects. They will have many desires to travel, but they will not have enough money to do it.

Those who are employed will receive a salary increase due to a change of position with more responsibility within the same job. This will allow them to broaden their professional experience. If they decide to change jobs or for those who are looking for a job, they will find a good opportunity.

As for money, they will have some major expenses, but they will know how to control their budget well. They will not have much money left for vacations, but they will make some getaways.

You will have to change your lifestyle; recent experiences have shown you that the way you live your life is not the right one. You will have to change your diet, exercise, and have a hobby that makes you feel happy. That will be especially important for their balance.

For singles, 2024 will be a momentous year. Love will be on the surface, and you will fall in love. Do not be in a hurry and live every moment slowly, getting to know the other person little by little. Without rushing. You will also experience many changes in your home and with your family members.

In general, 2024 will be a positive, happy year with many opportunities if you know how to improvise. You will achieve more than one purpose and move in the direction you want to go if you manage to stay in action.

The end of the year is when the biggest changes will occur, due in part to the ambitious plans you will have. You might move house or change the furniture. It will be crazy, but it is your greatest illusion.

Combination of the Zodiac Signs with the Chinese Horoscope Signs

When you combine Eastern and Western horoscopes, it is amazing how connected and accurate they are.

Chinese and Western horoscopes are the most used horoscopes. If you have the possibility to understand them deeply this will make it easier for you to use them and have a centralized approach.

Both horoscopes are based on the position of the stars, but in the Chinese horoscope 28 constellations are used, and in the western horoscope 88. The Chinese horoscope is based on 12 animals that rule each year, and the Western horoscope is based on 12 signs that rule each month.

The Chinese horoscope is based on the lunar calendar, and is the oldest horoscope known to date. Your zodiac sign matches your sign in the Chinese horoscope, but that does not happen often. If that were the case the predictions would be more accurate.

 There is an equivalence between the signs of both horoscopes:

Aries/Dragon, Taurus/Snake, Gemini/Horse, Cancer/Goat, Leo/Monkey, Virgo/Rooster, Libra/Dog, Scorpio/Pig, Sagittarius/Rat, Capricorn/Ox, Aquarius/Tiger, and Pisces/Rabbit.

Combinations

Rat

Aries/Rat

The blending of these signs results in a personality unique to their natures. The obsession and passion of Aries are buffered by the caution and perception of the Rat.

The person with this combination is perceptive, shrewd, and affable. He always has strategies to solve any situation and is hardly surprised by life's obstacles.

He is not a coward and likes challenges, which he overcomes with ease. This individual is worthy of admirations, because he knows how to improvise in any circumstance, counting on a will of steel.

Taurus/ Rat

The mixture of these two Taurus/Rat signs is beneficial, they are good friends, and they have an optimism to the skies. They are very honest and affable, distinguished by their tact in conversations.

The certainty of the Taurus sign combined with the irritation of the Rat is an excellent combination because it results in a unique magnetism. They are very thrifty and always have their feet on the ground. Their personality is enthusiastic, and they know how to be loyal.

Gemini /Rat

The mixture of these two signs results in a very cheerful person as they love adventures and risk. They always like to be busy and do not waste time on trifles. They adapt easily to any environment and hate to be alone.

The vitality of the Rat combined with the versatility of Gemini results in a very curious person. Sometimes they do not finish their goals because they put too much energy into the beginning of a plan.

Cancer/Rat

The mix of these two Cancer/Rat signs results in someone who is overly sensitive and always has dreams and goals. They are very selective with their friendships but have a good sense of humor.

Their mind is very perceptive and sharp and observation, subtly they can observe all the details in any situation. Having such a strong intuition they always decide correctly. They know very well how to accomplish their objectives because they never set impossible goals. Although they are dreamers, they always stick to their ideas.

Leo/Rat

The mix of these two Leo/Rat signs results in a person who is very self-centered and always needs to prove that they are the best. They love to be in positions of power and go out of their way to demonstrate their authority.

Sometimes the mysterious Rat forces Leo to be a hermit and be quiet. This is a very conflicting combination. Often the Rat/Leo person is incredibly famous, and their figure never goes unnoticed. Everyone is attracted by charisma and wants to be close to this person.

Virgo/ Rat

The mixture of these two signs is characteristic of courageous people who passionately believe in their simplicity. They are not anxious, they are perceptive, polite, and moderate in expressing their emotions.

They are very elegant and take great care of their personal appearance. They are implacable with the mistakes of others and detest people who do not strive to fulfill their purposes.

Libra /Rat

The Libra/Rat combination results in very pleasant, gentle people. Their behavior is courteous, and they are very tactful in their treatment of others.

You can trust them because they will never pull you down. The Libra's tact, combined with the Rat's attractiveness, gives these individuals a special charisma.

They are charming people who unfailingly attract attention. Communicating with these individuals always leaves you with a very pleasant feeling. They are very reasonable and practical; with their wisdom they will give you the best advice.

Scorpion/ Rat

This combination results in people with courage, and who inspire respect. Scorpio is a very manipulative and controlling sign, but with the wisdom of the Rat, they are indestructible in the face of any opposing enemy. They have an unmistakable nose for who is who, they have an unbreakable will and for them the word impossible does not exist in the dictionary.

They always act very quickly because they have decision-making power and do not waste their time on unnecessary things.

Sagittarius/Rat

The Sagittarius/Rat combination results in individuals with a lot of energy and vitality, but in a hurry to live life. These are the people that 24 hours a day are not enough to accomplish all their goals. They are always happy, and never complain about anything. Sagittarius' instability perfects the Rat's diligence, leading them to dislike routine.

They are overly optimistic and stand firm in their ideas. They use their reasoning to solve their problems and could offer the best advice.

Capricorn/Rat

The Capricorn/Rat combination results in a person who knows how to take care of his prestige and never gets involved in gossip.

They have a lot of dignity, and always strive to make the right impression. Capricorn's coldness fully compensates for the Rat's impetus.

They are sober and know how to control their emotions. They are educated, intelligent, and know how to behave in any social environment.

Aquarius/ Rat

The Aquarius/Rat combination results in people with an incredible imagination, and who are never bored. The extravagance of Aquarius, combined with the cautiousness of the Rat, offers a very peculiar temperament. These people, although friendly, are sometimes stubborn.

They are eternal lovers and protectors of their freedom, insightful and with high artistic potentials.

Pisces/Rat

This combination results in restless and sensitive people. The Rat gives them the ability to use their mind Rationally, and they are not discouraged by difficulties.

Although these people sometimes have moments of crisis when they become fragile, they are friendly, even withdrawn. They are very receptive, and act with caution so as not to commit imprudence. They do not tolerate laziness and injustice.

Ox

Aries/Bull

This combination results in very stubborn people. Aries increases their self-confidence, creating a rigid personality. These individuals are vain and conceited. They do not like to respect authority and sometimes it is better not to even have a discussion with them because they like to win no matter what.

They are determined and reasonable people, they calculate each of their steps because they have a bulletproof confidence. They are very emotional beings, for that reason most of their actions are conditioned by circumstances.

Taurus/ Ox

This mixture brings to the surface the most positive qualities of each sign, giving rise to tenacious and stubborn people. They possess self-confidence and are not capricious. They never change their minds and are not treacherous, they are affable with others, and loyal. It can be said that they have no faults, except that they are a little stubborn. They are never discouraged by life's obstacles because they know that every day is an opportunity to begin again.

Gemini/ Ox

This mix results in a person full of vitality and energy, someone who is always happy to be in this world. They are imaginative, and competent at solving urgent problems. They are distinguished by their physical toughness, and for them there is no mission impossible and no walls they cannot break down. The most embarrassing trials do not break their will. They are always cheerful, and this makes them have many friends who appreciate them for their good humor and positive aura.

Cancer/ Ox

The combination of these two signs gives rise to a rare temperament with some contradictions. They are not decisive, but they are very calm. They do their best to go unnoticed and prefer to watch from afar the unexpected, rather than act.

They are dreamers and harmless. They have a very acute intuition, and they value their faculties moderately. They can be highly organized and that is why their lives are successful.

Leo/ Ox

The mixture of these two signs results in proud people who dream of being famous all the time. These individuals proceed with dignity, and do not like to be cheated or deceived. They have principles and values, which is why they win the sympathy of others. They are funny and charming, but arrogant and selfish. They die stoically defending their points of view, and always find a tactful way to win.

They superbly combine politeness with self-confidence to get what they want, and so they surround themselves with calm people who are willing to accept their authority.

Virgo/O Ox

This combination results in focused and responsible people.

They are stubborn, but sociable and discreetly cautious. They are not cowards, and they are the kind of people who will always help you in any circumstance. They are vain people, and they always manage to find the place that belongs to them in this life.

Libra/Bull

People with this combination are wise and will never decide unless they have everything well thought out and calculated.

They prefer to act slowly, but with sure steps. The Ox's strength offers Libra self-confidence so that it does not perish in the face of doubts. At the same time, Libra sweetens the Ox's stubbornness, and its desire to control everyone.

You will always see them calm, and they are very polite. They try to please everyone and give service to those in need.

Scorpion/ Ox

This combination gives independent and bold people. They never ask for advice or help.

The perseverance of Scorpio, combined with the fearlessness of the Ox, gives these people amazing strength and power. Luck always favors these individuals who know how to take advantage of any opportunity.

They have a strong intuition, and although they are not the politest, they can show kindness when required.

Sagittarius / Ox

People with this combination are super fun to be around and are always willing to listen and help. The Ox's serious temperament balances the adventurous personality of Sagittarius, giving birth to individuals who are not reckless. They are calm, and their self-esteem is unalterable.

His circle of friends is extremely limited, he hates conflicts and scandals.

Capricorn/ Ox

The combination of these signs gives people obsessed with their profession and success. They can be insensitive and selfish, because the only thing they focus on is being famous and getting recognition. They are stubborn, self-sacrificing and plan their lives down to the last detail. They do not like anyone meddling in their lives and they do not like it when you give them an opinion or advice.

They are so confident that they will never listen to criticism, even if it is constructive.

Aquarius/ Ox

This mix gives individuals with an optimistic attitude. They love to travel, and when you are with them everything feels very peaceful. They are honest and loyal, with a super creative imagination. They move through this world with ease, ignoring any obstacles or problems that come their way.

They go through life easily, without paying attention to problems and difficulties. They live in a fantasy world and when they fall from the cloud they collide with a sometimes-unpleasant reality. Nevertheless, they have a solid character, and resist all crises with honor.

Pisces/ Ox

People with this combination easily resolve any conflict.

Although they are shy, they always find strength to overcome their weaknesses. They are skillful, helpful, and loyal. Their kindness knows no bounds. They are honest with those around them, and do not know how to pretend. This does not mean that they do not know how to defend themselves; if you happen to harm them, be prepared to suffer the consequences.

Tiger

Aries/ Tiger

This combination is typical of the most energetic people in existence. They do not rest even when they sleep because their time is valuable in every way. They are highly intelligent and ambitious, and always find a way to achieve their goals.

Quietness is their enemy because they need to be in constant movement. They never feel fear or doubt, they simply move forward with courage. They get along well with their friends, exhibiting a charming and affable personality.

Taurus /Tiger

This combination gives a temperamental person, who is always trying not to show his emotions. Overly cautious, they can lose control if confronted with injustice. Although Taurus restrains the stubborn energy of the Tiger, you should never impose your opinion on them. They are even-tempered and protect their honor with great caution.

Gemini/ Tiger

This mixture gives people with a wellspring of ideas and projects, often unattainable. They are very thoughtless but are endowed with great vitality and enthusiasm. The courage of the Tiger protects Gemini from rash decisions. They are fearless individuals and always look at everything that happens to them with an optimistic lens. They are always willing to experiment because they are not afraid of risks.

They have an inexhaustible source of energy to materialize all their plans.

Cancer/Tiger

Here, opposites collide, power and laziness, courage, and fragility. This struggle has an extraordinarily strong clash in the life of these individuals.

These are people with unpredictable temperaments, and for that reason they suffer pitifully from the most insignificant difficulties. They are insecure and always hesitating, as they are very reserved and do not ask or accept advice from anyone.

Leo/ Tiger

This union is extraordinarily strong and powerful. They are invulnerable, they are not afraid of anything or anyone. They are ambitious and always act with boldness and precision.

They are enveloping and charismatic, they know how to win the love and friendship of everyone. Despite their pride, they never hesitate to be kind.

Virgo/ Tiger

This mixture gives a sensitive person, a model of perfection. His behavior is perfect, causing fascination and respect. You can trust him, because when he helps you, he does it from his heart.

He never concentrates on the negative, on the contrary, he always tries to support you with a polite word. This is a psychologist and a master of life with the faculty to see the essence of things. With joy he always knows that there is a solution to every problem.

Libra/Tiger

Friendly, gentle, and courteous Libras/Tigers are excellent conversationalists. Being in their company is not only pleasant, but also safe. They will never offend with a rude word, they will understand, comfort, and certainly give valuable advice. Noble and strong Tiger is inferior to the diplomatic Libra, prone to long thoughts. Therefore, people of this sign are less energetic, but more thoughtful and balanced than the rest of the Tigers. They do not feel the need to impose their point of view, they do not spend their energy on trifles. But they are cheerful, joyful, they love to talk and surround themselves with beautiful things, nice people. Tigers/Libras strive for harmony in everything, they try to live in harmony with themselves and the world around them.

Scorpion/Tiger

This combination gives individuals of a rebellious and frantic will. Each of these signs is super self-sufficient and this makes the person determined. They are convinced that they are successful and positively welcome any change.

They are worthy of your trust because they possess a heart of honey. Their honesty and their desire to serve bring happiness to all those around them.

Sagittarius /Tiger

This mixture gives people who detest anxiety and depression. They are too optimistic to get entangled in such sad thoughts. They have a talent for overcoming difficulties and are always cheerful.

People love them because they are very sociable and friendly, and they have an ability to accept criticism with grace. Nothing in this world alters the youthful character of these people.

Capricorn / Tiger

When these two signs are conjugated, the person has a strong control over himself. All difficulties are dealt with calmly and intelligently.

In his manual of conduct there is no word betrayal, he is exceedingly kind, polite and helpful. He distrusts in occasions and that is the reason he shows a shy appearance.

Aquarius/ Tiger

This combination sweats joy, being near him gives a lot of peace and happiness. He is optimistic, inspires confidence and is very much loved. He copes with being alone and does not seek support. Aquarius is creative, has an unconventional mentality.

Tiger qualities are neutralized when they welcome Aquarian intellectuality. They think freely and never strive for power.

Pisces/ Tiger

These people fear change, are not worried about anything and are able to act decisively. They are sentimental and naturally generous, never feel envy and have an innate desire to serve those in need.

They are not naive, for that reason they will not help those who do not deserve it. They have an immense intuition that allows them not to make mistakes in their actions. They are very reserved with their personal problems.

Rabbit

Aries/ Rabbit

From this combination is born a continually active individual, full of energy, and not afraid to take risks. He is attracted to danger, can achieve his goals without the help and approval of others.

Never think of ignoring them, because, although they are charming, they are inflexible.

Taurus/Rabbit

This combination gives a calm person who values above all things his comfort. He never meddles in what does not concern him, he thinks that everyone is the master of his life and his problems.

They are diplomatic by nature, and tolerant of other people's imperfections. In their life there is no room for absurd problems and superficial concerns. Excessively perspicacious to spend their energy on trivial things. The union of Taurus and Rabbit is a proportionate mixture of integrity and sympathy.

Gemini/ Rabbit

These people are noticed in any environment because they have good tastes, which is why they always project an impressive personality. They love to be admired, and although they are thoughtful, they do not tolerated boredom. The Rabbit helps the restless part of Gemini to avoid accelerated actions. The combination of these signs is typical of people with an unconventional temperament. They communicate well and are loyal.

Cancer/ Rabbit

From this mixture comes a wise individual. However, he is unstable, stubborn, and materialistic. He thinks he is always right and thinks that everyone must respect him. For these people, the simplest failure is a misfortune since he is used to be deceived. That does not mean that he does not value himself, he knows how to get out of such circumstances with courage and tenacity.

Leo/ Rabbit

Luck is in favor of this type of person. The honesty of the Rabbit molds the pride of Leo, so this mixture gives discreet and educated individuals. They are very correct, attentive, have good manners and detest the hustle and bustle and harsh environments.

They are creative, never get bored, even if they are alone, and are always involved in new projects. Wherever you find them, they are remarkable for their charisma and their magnetic aura.

Virgo /Rabbit

This is a mixture that gives people that uncertainty creates intense states of anxiety. The union of the tender Rabbit, and Virgo is successful, because it achieves a harmony and balance out of series.

People with this combination have a measured lifestyle, avoiding any conflict whenever possible. They are unstable and are always happy with what they have. They enjoy the simple things in life, because for them being perfectionists is a very uncertain occupation.

Libra /Rabbit

It is a little hard to resist this attractive combination. Their polite temperament and the way they communicate will make anyone fall in love.

They are not rancorous and are not afraid to make fun of themselves. Libra's diplomacy in alliance with the Rabbit's balance gives these people even more finesse. They do not get involved in any argument and if it should happen, they always find a way to solve any difficulty.

For them, emotional health comes first, and everything else is secondary.

Scorpio/ Rabbit

This is a very sincere combination, which tends to be always pleasant. However, at the same time it is difficult. They have an intense energy that attracts and bewitches. They always act cautiously, displaying a unique set of skills. These individuals are incredibly lucky, all their business dealings always achieve success, and this often makes others very envious.

Sagittarius/ Rabbit

This individual is a wonderful communicator and a respectful listener. Always polite, they only think positive in any situation. They love to travel, and their lives are full of interesting stories.

The qualities of the Rabbit soften the independent character of Sagittarius. The effect of the union of these two signs is excellent, in fact, it is said to be the most famous and triumphant combination of the twelve fusions.

Capricorn / Rabbit

From this combination comes a calm and balanced individual. The Capricorn's stubbornness and seriousness are a fantastic match for the

Rabbit's delicacy and uncertainty. This results in a person who stands out for his independent temperament.

He is romantic, but only with his family and friends. The union of Capricorn and Rabbit justifies his talent, and the potential for adaptation in any circumstance.

Aquarius/ Rabbit

From this combination comes an unpredictable individual, who is not afraid to look eccentric. A lover of freedom, this person thinks that it is not important to join the usual rules.

They have an excellent character, are cheerful and optimistic. This combination has a natural spirit of adventure, and you will never see them sad or discouraged.

Pisces/ Rabbit

The gentlest individuals come out of this combination. Although outwardly innocent, that is part of their ability to be polite, and not a representation of their soul. These people are intuitive and insightful, but also shrewd, so no one can take advantage of them.

This union results in manipulative people who know how to deal with weaknesses.

Dragon

Aries / Dragon

This combination results in a vigorous person. Obstacles do not exist for him. Life endowed him with the faculties of a true leader. Sometimes they are impulsive and have little tolerance for the shortcomings of others.

As an enemy, they are cruel, self-confident, very vain. They never consider the opinions of others and strive for greatness at any cost and under any circumstances.

Taurus/Dragon

These people are very balanced. The stamina of the Taurus sign combined with the intense energy of the Dragon, is prone to extravagant actions.

This is an intelligent, down-to-earth individual. At the same time, he is cheerful, and loves to spoil himself with little trifles. However, he never wastes his energy in vain.

Gemini/ Dragon

These people are energetic and always find ways to realize their fantasies. They are incredibly lucky, because of their intuition they perceive very subtly the energies that surround them.

A person of this combination is distinguished not only by his knowledge and joviality, but also by his maturity. He is a dynamic and incredibly famous person. He is endowed with many abilities, but the most significant is his subtlety.

Cancer/Dragon

This is an individual who is always prepared, appreciates people, and truly rejoices in their triumphs. This Cancer is not as sensitive as the rest. The Dragon gives him power and self-confidence.

He has an even temper and does not commit rash acts. Methodical and calm, he can challenge decisively. He is stubborn, fickle, and tactless.

Leo / Dragon

This is an individual who is a born achiever. Failure and defeat do not exist for him. He is intelligent, and confident that is why he solves any problem. The union of Leo and Dragon is a phenomenally successful combination that endows the person with an unusual attractiveness. His life is successful, and he can easily achieve everything he wants.

Virgo/ Dragon

This person is strong, prefers to solve all problems, and not get lost in nonsense. He possesses a grandiose imagination and is a person with a complex character. He gives the impression of being calm, but really dreams of glory.

This is an idealist who strives for perfection with confidence. In short, he is an extraordinary and unique person.

Libra/ Dragon

The individual with this combination is discreet and intelligent. Behind his charming personality hides a strong temperament. Limited in communication, he protects his inner world from external curiosities. He is distinguished by his good will, being energetic and vigorous.

He is always attentive to other people's problems, however, due to his delicacy he cannot go through other people's misfortunes. Although he enjoys solitude, he sometimes needs friends.

Scorpio/Dragon

These people live according to their own convictions because they do not have the ability to adapt to other people's standards. They are very self-sufficient, do not like to complain and much less curse their luck.

The power of the Dragon's fire gives him strength, and Scorpio's tenacious nature does not allow him to stop fighting and falling. He has a very great courage, a person difficult to discern, and impossible to tame.

Sagittarius/Dragon

This mix gives the world cheerful and optimistic people who know how to enjoy life. The most outstanding characteristic of the Sagittarius sign is its optimism, the Dragon shares its strength with it. This person is prepared for any experience. This is one of the most compassionate Dragons, his strength can only be the cause of envy.

He has the faculty to encourage, for that reason he is always surrounded by friends.

Capricorn/Dragon

This is the person who is confident that he will always succeed. He is not afraid of losing because he knows that failures are lessons and steppingstones to move forward.

He is modest and dignified, never asks for mercy, achieving all his goals through his work, differentiating himself by his efficiency. He combines the qualities of both signs, practicality, courage, and secrecy. This is a natural winner, with vigorous energy and extraordinary charisma.

Aquarius/Dragon

This combination gives an extraordinary person with incomparable creativity. He seeks freedom to be able to live as he wants and is an eternal dreamer. It is very normal for him to make mistakes, although sometimes it is exceedingly difficult for him to see his own mistakes. Under the influence of the Dragon, Aquarius acquires sanity. People of this combination are famous for their versatility, and for suffering sudden changes of character.

Pisces/ Dragon

A fragile and defenseless person comes out of this combination. It is a distrustful, cautious, and strict individual.

They are characterized by always having doubts, however, sometimes they are capable of risky actions, if they must defend themselves. There are many mysteries in these people, but their primary traits are frankness and spontaneity.

Snake

Aries / Snake

This is a person with extraordinary willpower. He is slow and methodical, and never trusts other people's opinion. His attitude of being prudent and always intuiting what is best in each situation stands out.

The wise Snake gives Aries the gift of intuition and thus guarantees success. Their decisions are always precise and timely, they obtain with ease everything they plan. They have an incredible ability to influence the destiny of other people.

Taurus /Snake

These people give the impression of being positive people, but in need of affection. They are loved for their balanced temperament. They have infinite patience and for that reason they always accomplish their goals.

The union between the striving Taurus and the intelligent Snake is successful, it is an energy reinforced with pragmatism, serenity, and reasonableness.

Gemini/ Snake

These are people full of enthusiasm and optimism. Despite their versatility they are not superficial, but rather prone to abstraction and reasoning.

People of this combination are organized, which is not characteristic of the Gemini sign. The union of the Snake and Gemini is interesting as these two signs enhance each other. However, they can be demanding.

Cancer /Snake

This union gives a mysterious individual. The main peculiarity is his intuition. He does not tolerate unpleasant criticism about himself, although he is an attractive and funny person who knows how to please others.

He is highly intelligent, sensitive, and correct, therefore, conversations with him are full of positive energies.

Leo /Snake

This mixture gives individuals lacking in pragmatism. They actively participate in other people's lives. It is an extraordinarily strong person who always requires excessive requirements. They think they are the last coke in the desert, therefore, they are always complaining to others, although they do it with tact and diplomacy.

He is a very sociable, communicative, polite person, but he carefully hides his true feelings.

Virgo/ Snake

This combination results in a calm person who instills confidence in others. It is remarkable not only her external beauty but also her good manners and education. She has a super developed intuition and a methodical mind. She dedicates a lot of time to reflect to be able to draw conclusions.

He is a bit of a quiet person, but when he communicates, he is interesting as he enjoys joking and sharing neutral topics.

Libra/Snake

That is the most diplomatic individual on the face of the earth. It is a famed mix because these people are very calm and even-tempered. They are super polite, and they respect the opinions of others.

They do not require outside approval because they are very self-confident. They are easy to have a good relationship with, they are optimistic about the future, and with their charm they attract all kinds of people into their lives.

However, they are not as innocent as they seem, their wisdom passes all limits, and their views are otherworldly.

Scorpio/Snake

This mixture is prone to unpredictable actions. Their will is extraordinarily strong.

It is impossible to confuse this combination because they always act in accordance with their own ideals. It exclusively does what it thinks is necessary, and in the process afflicts others. Everyone around her must submit to her will, and if they do otherwise you become her enemy. Simultaneously she seeks her inner peace.

Sagittarius /Snake

This combination is the most attractive and sociable of all the Snakes. It is charismatic, but full of contradictions. It is intelligent, and insightful, but with the capacity to make rash decisions, because it is also emotional and impulsive.

Those around him hardly ever understand them, nor do they approve of his bizarre lifestyle.

Capricorn/Snake

This person has a developed intellect, is sensible and has a frightening cold-bloodedness. He is indifferent to others, and never needs their support.

She sometimes reacts angrily when she is criticized. She has a super gifted mind, and always calculates any situation in advance. She is very controlled, she never has the luxury of emotions overpowering her, but of course she has many flaws that make her an ordinary person.

Aquarius /Snake

This mix spends his life longing for new experiences. This combination is sympathetic as it is an efficient person with transformational thinking.

They have prominent skills and incomparable aptitudes. The most important thing for them is not to look like anyone else. They have an energy with such magnitude that they easily overcome any obstacle.

Pisces /Snake

Here we have a moderate and educated person. Considered a model of justice.

The Snake gives you respectability, power, and firmness. It is distinguished by its courtesy and patience, but also by its whims and its desire for revenge if you get in its way. It is very effusive and wishes to live passions 24 hours a day.

Horse

Aries / Horse

These people have an irrepressible energy, and they are very curious. This combination invigorates the characteristics of both signs. The Aries sign is stubborn and tenacious. This is a Horse with an uncontrollable temper.

This is an emotional person, but not afraid of changes, on the contrary, always takes advantage of any circumstance to drastically transform his life.

Taurus/ Horse

This person does not care about anything in life, only about avoiding suffering and going his own way. He is not interested in changing the world and showing that he has unique qualities.

He is a person of strong temperament, knows what he needs, and what he wants, from life, and plans to obtain it with great peace and tranquility. Stubborn, inflexible, he fears nothing because he lacks weaknesses. He is a noble and sensitive person covered with the armor of the Knights Templar.

Gemini /Horse

These are fast people, full of ideas and plans. They are identified by their unpredictable personality, as they easily change their opinions.

Never get bored because they are usually surrounded by friends. It is illusory to prophesy their moods, or to understand the motives behind their actions.

Cancer/ Horse

These people are humble, sensitive, and depend a lot on the criteria of others. Cancer is a withdrawn sign by nature, but under the domination of the Horse they become confident.

These individuals have a harmoniously balanced personality, which confers them self-control, and the faculty to contain the negative expressions of their nature.

Leo/ Horse

These people infest others with their optimism because they love life in all its manifestations. They do not know how to be sad and think positively in any circumstance.

He never doubts any person and goes to great lengths to fulfill the wishes of all his family and friends. They try to use logical thinking, but do not exclude the influence of emotions. Sometimes they face setbacks, but these circumstances do not affect their moods.

Virgo/ Horse

These individuals are seductive and positive. Their temperament is balanced, they are active, and energetic. The union of these two signs is very fruitful because it endows these people with optimism.

They know how to enjoy life and stand out for their joy. They are always striving to evolve and acquire new knowledge. They usually succeed wherever they go.

Libra/ Horse

This combination gives cheerful people of a super affable temperament. They do not like to be alone and make friends quite easily. They have a lot of self-control; their mentality is very developed and other people forgive them easily. Some if they expose their negative side can be narcissistic or have a bad temper.

Scorpio/ Horse

This individual is exceedingly difficult to deal with because he is stubborn. He is an enthusiastic person, not afraid of conflict, and is very self-confident. Sometimes he is very selfish and behaves like a child when he is not given a toy.

They perceive each other's pain and have a propensity to avoid them if those people are close to them.

Sagittarius/ Horse

This individual has a unique naivety, he is incredibly happy and enjoys every moment. He lives in the here and now.

He is overly optimistic, and a dreamer. He abhors boredom, he is like a child, who perseveres to learn everything incognito. There can be nothing intact in his life, everything must unfold in a cycle of change, whether it is a change in family status, work, or home.

Capricorn/Horse

These individuals are realistic and fearless. These people plan their future carefully, they are tenacious with a high potential for creativity and a lot of reasoning.

They achieve everything they set out to do, and their sociable nature is very influential in their family circle. He is receptive, and people tell him their problems because they always receive appropriate advice.

Aquarius/ Horse

This person is persevering and born to succeed. He is very curious and cannot stand laziness. His life is in constant change and for this reason he sometimes gets a little angry. The unpredictable Horse exalts Aquarius characteristics such as joy, and restlessness. These people are always in a hurry and are afraid that time will run out and they will not be able to finish everything they planned. He is firmly confident in his victory; he is distinguished by his fanciful.

Pisces/ Horse

These people are easy-going and easily win the sympathy of everyone they meet. They are known for their affable character and make friends easily.

They are funny and empathize with the pain of others. They are always willing to support anyone, even those they do not know.

Goat

Aries/ Goat

This individual is strong and determined. He is stubborn and does not care much about other people's problems. He is ambitious and perseveres to succeed.

People of this combination are always active, doing something or waiting for something. It is exceedingly kind and refuses to believe in human malice.

Taurus /Goat

These people are distinguished by their cheerful outlook. From time to time, they step back to think calmly about important problems. They cannot stand the fuss, act with prudence and deliberation.

They solve any conflict by reasoning, to avoid useless losses. They do not spend money without thinking twice and have a very advanced intelligence and intuition.

Gemini/ Goat

These people are affable and captivate others with their indefatigable cheerfulness. They prefer a family atmosphere, being away from the hustle and bustle and detest gossipy people.

You can trust them because they are an honest person, they do not know how to lie and cheat. They are intelligent and try to achieve success in any project. They are not prone to squandering, but they help their relatives financially and with advice.

Cancer/ Goat

This is a kind, accommodating person. He always avoids conflict and is super skilled at hiding his discontent. He is vulnerable but is overly cautious despite his mental weakness.

He carefully protects his personal space, his home is his sanctuary, and there he takes refuge when he is in trouble. He is known for his ability to respond sincerely, but with kindness.

Leo / Goat

These people like to be the center of attention, are worthy of admiration and have wisdom.

When they work, it is always to achieve a high goal. Their wisdom and perspicacity help them to avoid mistakes, and in emergencies they can resort to incredibly wise strategies. They like luxury and know how to live with elegance.

Virgo/ Goat

This is a very sensible person. He can think logically and is pragmatic in business.

They are Rational but can also be capricious and unstable. They love to comment and give advice, and they have an innate talent for seeing any defect, so they supervise in detail their actions and those of their colleagues. The people around them admire their efforts and treat them with respect. These individuals usually have no enemies.

Libra/ Goat

These people are very sociable and are kind to others. They have many hidden talents but are inclined towards the arts. They like luxurious things, and to be accompanied by elegant people. They try to maintain a reasonable balance, and not to fall into baseness. They can carry their responsibility to others. They adapt easily to changes and perceive positively any transformation.

Scorpio/ Goat

These people have an extraordinary intuition, they easily distinguish false people, and it is impossible to lie to them. They are loyal people,

They are not mean, they try to brave, and, but simultaneously have doubts and are tormented by their insolvency. So cautiously guard their secrets so carefully that no one can penetrate the depths of their soul.

Sagittarius/ Goat

This is the person who is always up to date with the latest development. He is insightful, and ambitious with everything new. He has unconventional thinking, and sometimes surprises others with his unforeseen actions.

They deftly avoid obstacles, always have a Plan B ready, because their shrewd mentality helps them in tricky situations. They do not like to give themselves extra obligations, and sometimes they are good counselors.

Capricorn /Goat

This is a mix where perseverance is synonymous with these people. They are not afraid of anything, and never give up, even if things get serious. These individuals are unlikely to give up, and they plan and calculate everything in detail.

They are never offended by any criticism and know how to sweeten any person with bad character. They defend the truth to the last consequences, even if it goes against their interests.

Aquarius / Goat

These people are absolutely focused on their feelings, they are honest, they are loquacious, able to communicate their opinions to everyone.

He is an emotional person, who feels beauty very lightly. It has never been in his plans to let strangers into his private life because it is much more comfortable for him to keep good relations, and not to be attached to everyone. He loves to share with his relatives. He plans his general budget sensibly, is not greedy, and does not spend money on nonsense.

Pisces / Goat

People with this combination have a calm character. They appreciate comfort, love their home, and are very connected to their family members. Sometimes they idealize their friends, expect understanding, and help from them in tough times. They do not tolerate lies and betrayal. They have an emphasized sense of justice and strictly do not accept cruelty. They successfully combine business and pleasure.

Monkey

Aries /Mono

People with these signs are persuasive. These individuals like to laugh. They explore the world with enthusiasm and joy, and they are also very inquisitive.

They are not responsible and careful with business, but being so active they usually succeed. They are confident in their abilities, but if they fail, they get angry with everyone, including themselves. The worst humiliation for them is to be left behind. They do not listen to other people's criticism but are susceptible to it.

Taurus/ Monkey

This is a combination of power. People with these signs are sociable and possess infinite optimism. They are someone you can trust; under any situation they keep their mind positive.

You are unconcerned about money and are not interested in speculation. You are successful in business, and do not need to try as hard as the other signs. You always put the interests of the people you love first and sacrifice for them.

Gemini /Mono

This combination of signs gives impulsive and restless people. You can communicate very easily with them, and emotions never get in the way of doing the right thing.

They are enthusiastic, with an intense desire to progress. They know the techniques to defeat their enemies. They can remain under pressure for a long time and the influence of the Gemini sign transforms them into a versatile person.

Cancer /Mono

These people have a sharp mind. They possess an enigmatic personality, but with the capacity to feel deeply. These individuals are characterized by living suffocated by their feelings, listening to their intuition. They are a little shy, but at the same time insatiable and self-confident. They are distrustful when they must start a love relationship, they are afraid of being hurt. They are unstable with their temperament and for that reason they never have noticeably clear ideas to keep their life in order.

Leo/ Monkey

This person is very receptive. They are leaders par excellence; they know where they want to go and for that goal, they put all their dedication.

They are not afraid of obstacles, rather they are strengthened by them. They are idealistic and insightful. They can be a little stubborn in their opinions, but always maintain an unconditional sincerity. They are attracted to luxury and power. They can use traps to disgrace their enemies. They can also assume arrogant behaviors.

Virgo/ Monkey

This is a complex combination. They act diplomatically and without reservation. They are very discreet, but fun. They enjoy helping other people solve their problems.

They are charming, like to learn and can analyze the most complicated contexts. They are so observant and intuitive that they can see all sides of an issue. They are practical, willful, and astute, always looking for excellence. They possess the gift of prudence.

Libra /Mono

These people have a big heart. They get involved in the problems of others because they feel them. They detest injustice and are very sociable. They do not tolerate cruelty; they are very diplomatic in the face of hostilities. They like to work in teams, they are curious, a virtue that when they use it to discover new things is beneficial, but it can also become a defect if it gives them to meddle in the affairs of others. They never make false steps because they never lose elegance. They are a mixture of exquisiteness and dynamism.

Scorpion/ Monkey

These are the signs of multifaceted people. They are people with clairvoyant abilities, they are mysterious and independent. They usually like to create a shield to protect their emotions.

They are bohemian individuals, and although they are detached from the world, they are judging with their critical mentality. They are powerful, their willpower is incredible, yet they are easily afflicted by the conditions around them. They do not know how to keep their mouths shut, becoming overly critical. They are good friends with people they consider worthy of respect.

Sagittarius/ Monkey

This combination is typical of versatile and adventurous people. Their minds are always open to new experiences.

They are dependable, and are always willing to fight for worthy causes, even if it costs them their lives. They love to start projects and learn new things. They are particularly good organizers, and generous. They have a great temperament that appears in difficult circumstances.

Capricorn /Mono

The combination of these signs gives responsible individuals, willing to persevere to achieve their goals.

They are fair people, but their personality is sometimes introverted, and a little insecure. They are people you can trust; they are very respectful. They are excellent in administration and in everything related to economy. Expressing their feelings is sometimes extremely hard for them, however, when they give themselves, they are enthusiastic in intimacy.

Aquarius/ Monkey

Individuals with this combination are famous for their fantasies. They are super original and sincere.

Generous, and independent, making friends is vital to them, although their circle of friends is large and inconsistent. They are sociable and being busy with their friend is having fun is their priority. They are compassionate, when they give something, they do it selflessly. They usually shine in any profession that gives them the opportunity to use their talents.

Pisces /Mono

This combination is extremely interested in social problems, but they hate to be judged, and it is a great offense if someone criticizes them. They are never in a bad temper, and if this is the case, they do not project it. They treat everyone well, enjoy spending time with their friends, and are sociable. They are the perfect individuals when it comes to scheduling a social gathering, and they are always up for an enjoyable time.

They are transparent, and do not believe in human evil. They are easy for people to trust them.

Rooster

Aries / Rooster

These are the people who are determined and stubborn. Convincing them to change their minds can become an impossible mission.

They are autonomous and skillful in guiding their lives. Sometimes they are very stubborn when it comes to reaching an agreement when they have different points of view. When they fall in love, they are faithful and jealous, and want to be given all the attention. Their emotional displays are accelerated and intense. When other people are in difficulties, they are the first to offer their help.

Taurus /Gallo

This combination gives people moderation. Their temperament is extraordinarily strong, and versatile.

They are distinguished by their ability to respond to any circumstance where the environment is chaotic. They are practical, decisive and with great willpower. They are stable and always loyal to a trusted leader. They love tranquility and are respectful of rules. They avoid debt and are reluctant to change. They love luxury and tasty food.

Gemini/ Rooster

These people are free and like to openly express feelings. They are not afraid to be different, with the family is moderate.

They are sensual and faithful, good parents and tend to be possessive. They are enterprising and succeed in professions related to finance. Sometimes they use their qualities to obtain their own purposes and can resort to falsehood without losing their grace to get what they want. They are easily disheartened when they do not receive praise.

Cancer /Gallo

A person with these signs likes to be praised. His intuition is so developed that it allows him to understand the emotional states of other people. It is a confident person, communicative, and it is interesting to talk to him. They are cautious when it is necessary, they know how to identify with others because of their great imagination. They are vain and try to build their life according to a fantastic ideal. They are prone to be disorderly and like to be flattered. They have an excellent memory, and success as administrators.

Leo/ Rooster

These two signs together make for a charming person, but with an unconventional temperament. They never hesitate when a decision must be made and if they hesitate no one notices.

They are independent and calculating, characteristics that always help them to achieve what they set out to do. They know how to overcome any obstacle without fear. Their self-confidence sometimes leads them to stubbornness, showing their bad temper, power, and arrogance. Pride can control them at specific moments and even show naive attitudes that do not allow them to reason.

Virgo/ Rooster

This mixture gives intelligent, dependable, and honest people. They behave politely and can have any topic of conversation. They have an extraordinarily strong intuition, and their opinions are never biased.

He is sociable, understands and understands the feelings of others and they are eloquent. Sometimes they are too loquacious, but they know how to stop in time. They are astute and therefore know how to express their opinions. They are prone to criticize, something that makes others feel very offended.

Libra /Gallo

This mix of signs is possessed by people who never get upset over trifles. They are kind and calm people. The fusion of the Rooster and Libra creates a balanced personality. This combination is perfect because these people have a great power of seduction and are charming.

They never stop until they get the ideal result. They project a positive image, communicate with all types of people, and adapt to any circumstance.

Scorpion/ Rooster

The person with these signs is a leader par excellence. They can recognize the weaknesses of others, but do not criticize them because they know that no one is perfect. This individual sometimes has a complicated and difficult to understand character because they are also sometimes immensely proud and greedy. Sexual relationships can be their weakness, they have many partners during their life. They are honest with their partners if love lasts.

Sagittarius/ Rooster

These two signs fused together give a person who is the life of the party, and the best company. They love to be the center of attention, yet they are quiet and eloquent. They are honest, and although they are peaceful, they often meddle in conflicts, but never act maliciously.

This is the person who transmits optimism, knows how to apologize when he is wrong, and loves his family above all things.

Capricorn / Rooster

When these two signs meet, the person is talkative, but not about trivial matters. They are moderate with their actions because they do not like to harm anyone. Their stubbornness does not allow them, at times, to recognize their mistakes, and they are reluctant to compromise. Their patience is infinite and their will unbreakable, something that allows them to be decisive. Beneath this shield of equanimity hides their sensitivity. They know how to persuade with ease and with their charisma it is exceedingly difficult not to pay attention to them.

Aquarius/ Rooster

This combination is typical of eccentric and libertine people. Their personality is irresistible and their aura intriguing. They are not afraid to be dreamers because they are convinced that their ideas are the best, they are always involved in innovative projects and are ambitious.

They are good friends, considerate, and helping others is a priority for them. Although they rarely get involved in other people's problems, if there is an injustice, they will go out to defend the weakest, even if they must risk their lives.

Pisces /Gallo

This fusion gives people who see beauty in everything, they are individuals who are honest to the point of going against themselves. In their words there is music because they are educated, they are bold when it comes to telling the truth, although they express themselves with a lot of tact.

They are fighters and know how to develop a strategic plan to achieve their goals. They are very receptive to other people's pain, and they understand the emotions of others.

Dog

Aries / Dog

People with this combination of signs are restless. They are forerunners of justice and always can sacrifice themselves for others. They are very decent, have a high professional level and behave honestly with their friends.

These individuals have a good heart, their mind is very suspicious, and their intuition allows them to recognize when someone is deceiving them. They detest hypocritical people, and never engage in gossip.

Taurus /Dog

The mixture of these two signs gives reliable and dignified individuals. They are very responsible and noble. They like to see the positive side of any circumstance, and project confidence and kindness.

They are very patient, scrupulous and have high moral values. They know how to listen and never impose their opinions. They are tenacious in person, willful, and the tangible is a tool they always use to move forward.

Gemini/ Dog

A balanced individual is the result of the union of these two energies. Sometimes they are restless and lack emotional intelligence because they tend to have unpredictable behaviors.

They have a sophisticated temperament that motivates them to make hasty decisions and disappoint the people around them. They are easily offended, although they are sociable with a fraternally character. They do not support the routine; they are curious and active.

Cancer/ Dog

People with these signs are reserved. They have dual personalities because they are very protective of their surroundings. They live their lives with great passion and enjoy their family whom they always protect. They are prone to be carried away by temptations, indulgent with themselves sometimes they tend to be lazy and provocative.

They can easily be manipulated and that is the reason they must repress their doubts and isolate their emotions.

Leo/ Dog

These people are proud and self-confident. They never doubt themselves and are courageous. They enjoy being the center of attention, they are leaders and like to control everything. They are against injustice; their personality is magnetic, and they inspire others with their actions because they have a lot of courage.

They express what they think freely, they are realistic and protective. When they are betrayed, they move away and hold grudges, avoiding getting close to others.

Virgo /Dog

A combination that gives impeccable individuals with an iron resistance. They are gentle and practical; they never make mistakes when deciding because they have analyzed all the pros and cons. They are demanding with their friends, they choose people with high values, and who are honest. The possibility of rejection terrifies them, and this feeling prevents them from giving themselves completely to relationships. They often invent drama to fill the void when life becomes tedious.

Libra/ Dog

This combination gives kind people, with the ability to sacrifice their interests for the common good. They require all areas of their lives to be balanced to feel secure. They are their own worst adversary, as they evaluate this balance by provoking extreme situations. They are perceptive and attentive to others. They can focus, but that does not exempt them from committing reckless acts.

They rarely listen to advice, have varied interests, and a sense of competition makes them excellent in the creative area.

Scorpion/ Dog

This mixture gives an arrogant person. Really deep down they are overly sensitive and compassionate, but they do not show it because that is their protection mechanism. They are mystics, with a well-developed intuition, and a cautious sense of communication.

They are polite, faithful, and like to enjoy life to the fullest without stopping to think too much. They are charismatic and determined.

Sagittarius/ Dog

This is a person who never tolerates being alone. They are optimistic and speak their mind without restraint. They always attract others into their lives because of the positive energy they project, and for that reason their circle of friends grows daily.

In them you can trust, you will have a shoulder to cry on, and a hand to hold in the most terrible moments.

Capricorn/ Dog

This person is calm and intelligent. He is sociable, responsible, and compassionate. He is respectful, and with extremely high moral values. Once they fall in love, they are very faithful, but jealous. Lies have no place in their lives, so they trust everyone. They persevere tenaciously, and assume many responsibilities, they strive to be considered and respected by others. They know how to manage themselves financially, keeping in mind their aspirations and the best way to achieve them.

Aquarius/ Dog

These people are very responsible, and do not need the support of others. They value their opinion above those of others. They excel in any profession and know how to put themselves in the place of others as they are good friends. They often do not know how to recognize reality and can become obsessed with their perceptions.

He is endowed with superior intelligence, and therefore feels that the rest of the world is not up to his standards.

Pisces /Dog

These people tend to live in a cloud because they are dreamers. They will do anything to get money, which is why they can fall into a state of desperation that leads them to commit illegal acts. Because of their fear of confrontation, they often withdraw and become very vulnerable.

They repel discipline, love drama, and are capricious and intuitive. They are very suspicious, understand everything very well and are not selfish with their friends.

Pig

Aries / Pig

A combination that gives exceedingly kind and affable people. They are peaceful by birth; they hate problems and gossip. They avoid conflicts, they smell them from a distance. They are optimistic, have excellent mental and emotional health and ability to work hard.

They are accustomed to deceiving themselves in sentimental matters, and for that reason when they suffer a disappointment, they become a meringue. They are generous, they are in constant search of their soul mate and when they find it, they give themselves unconditionally.

Taurus / Pig

A mix that results in very accommodating people. They love to have fun, are cheerful and have a lot of patience. They are diligent workers and fighters, and kind-hearted. They are sometimes unpleasant when things do not happen the way they want them to. Their generosity is sometimes taken advantage of by unscrupulous people.

They are compassionate, methodical, and in tune with their emotions.

Gemini/ Pig

Combination brought into the world by people who are cheerful, but irresponsible. They cannot have obligations because they are overwhelmed.

They are always at odds with everyone and like to argue over petty things. They are jealous of their partners, controlling and insecure.

Their imagination is strong, they see ghosts where there are none, and their reputation is dubious.

Cancer/ Pig

Very self-sufficient people. They think they are the navel of the universe and like to be noticed by everyone. They fight for their success, and love fame.

He is cheerful, and balanced, but very vulnerable to criticism. They have sudden mood swings and are very sincere in expressing their emotions. For them it is essential to have money because they connect their emotional states to this energy.

Leo / Pig

These people are leaders, love the good life and will fight to have the comforts they think they deserve. However, they are very compassionate and kind. They are sensitive to other people's emotions and generous to family and friends. They know how to control their finances, can be self-centered and capricious.

They enjoy social and family gatherings where everyone gets together and enjoys their charismatic and attractive presence.

Virgo /Pig

This connection gives reasonable people. They are very discreet, and distrustful. They stand out for their altruism, and if they cannot help you, they will advise you. They become a stone of ice during conflicts, and momentarily may break down or accuse you of their ills. They can be pessimistic, and as they receive the support, they need they are prone to states of depression.

They persevere in what they want to achieve, are honest and do not like absurd objectives.

Pound /Pig

A combination that stands out for its insight. They never cross boundaries unless authorized to do so, whether with friends or partners. Brilliant at negotiations, and cautious in their opinions.

He does his best not to be involved in conflictive situations. He does not tolerated falsehoods, cheating and injustice.

Scorpion /Pig

These two signs are typical of people who seem naive but are highly intelligent. They like to analyze you to know what you can give them of benefit. They are selfish and vain. They have sophisticated strategies to win people's love and friendship. They are charismatic and enjoy being the center of attention.

They are planned, detest the unexpected, and go from happiness to sadness very easily.

Sagittarius /Pig

These two signs result in individuals who are compassionate and optimistic. They stand out for their honesty, and their repulsion to toxic people. They are people who when they have to say something do not beat around the bush, they are direct and appreciate that you are the same with them. They value the opinions of others; listen to the advice they receive with gratitude and have an enviable energy.

They achieve everything they set out to do because when they have a purpose, they put all their energies and focus into it.

Capricorn/ Pig

People with these signs are very relaxed, they go through life without tormenting themselves and know that there is always a second chance. They communicate openly and are very friendly. They are emotional, they are genuinely nice and with them you never get bored at a party as they always have something to tell.

Their temperament is strong, they are very dignified, you can trust them and if you tell them a secret, they will take it to the grave.

Aquarium /Pig

This combination exposes a tendency to out-of-this-world logical thinking. In general, they are very balanced people, and their mind is always active to look for the best solutions to any conflict situation.

They are kind people who enjoy giving you a hand, always recognize their faults and learn from experiences. They are known for having an X-Ray eye for any detail, and with this characteristic they are the right people for jobs that take this kind of skill,

Pisces /Pig

The combination of these signs is typical of people who have many spiritual values. They are peaceful and, in all circumstances, will go out of their way not to get involved in conflicts. They are not selfish and if they must go the extra mile for you, they will do it without a second thought.

They are diligent workers to be admired, they try their best, even if they are exhausted. They do not stop when they get tired, but when they finish.

Decorating your Home according to Feng Shui

Feng Shu is a Chinese philosophy that examines the environment, based on the theory of Yin and Yang and the Five Elements.

Experts have shown that areas in ancient China were regularly chosen in territories that are surrounded by mountains and had a river. It was not only because these areas provided the primary criteria for survival, but to comply with the patterns established by Feng Shui.

The main idea of Feng Shui is to achieve balance between humankind and the Universe. If there are good energies, there is balance, since Feng Shui affects the destiny of each person.

Through the study of Feng Shui, human beings can work on their compatibility with nature, their environment, and their lives, to achieve more prosperity and health in life.

Theory of the Five Elements

The theory of the Five Elements is a component of Feng Shui. These Elements are important in determining the proper Feng Shui in each space. These elements are Fire, Earth, Metal, Water and Wood, and each has a particularity that symbolizes specific aspects of life.

The Five Elements are the expression used by Feng Shui to explain the structure of nature, and these elements act together and must always be balanced.

Feng Shui for the Twelve Signs of the Chinese Horoscope

Sign of the Rat

Water favors people born under the sign of the Rat; it helps them to obtain prosperity. To obtain abundance, they should put a goldfish tank in the northern part of their office.

Sign of the Ox

People of this sign will achieve prosperity if they use the Fire element. To achieve this, they should place porcelain or ceramic articles in their businesses or offices, and in their homes.

Sign of the Tiger

The earth element is the one that individuals belonging to the sign of the Tiger should use. They should add something relevant that symbolizes this earth element. A potted plant, or a natural growing flower can bring prosperity to their lives.

Rabbit Sign

For luck and to attract abundance, people of the Rabbit sign require a secret earth element in their lives. You should hide a jade or Citrine quartz in the Northeast part of your home or office.

Dragon Sign

The Northwest is excellent for those who were born under the sign of the Dragon. In this direction they should place a bowl with clear water mixed with a little bit of earth. Another option is to place a Lotus Flower in a bowl.

Sign of the Snake

Prosperity will come into the lives of individuals belonging to the sign of the Snake if they use Metal objects, specifically Gold and Silver, in their home or offices.

Sign of the Horse

The Northwest is the recommended position for people of the sign of the Horse to obtain a great capital. They should place a Metal frog in the Northwest of their home or business.

Sign of the Goat

North is the appropriate cardinal point for people born under the sign of the Goat. They should place a small wooden box, or other wooden object, in the North of their office or home. If they use a wooden box, they should place an object related to their profession in it. For example, a writer can place a pencil in the box.

Monkey Sign

For prosperity to come into the lives of people born under the sign of the Monkey, they should place a plant of their size, or larger, in that cardinal point on the west side of the house or business.

Rooster Sign

Good luck will come to the life of those who belong to the Rooster sign, if they place some seeds in a glass, bottle, or bowl of dark red color. They should not use any Metal.

Dog Sign

People belonging to the sign of the Dog should dispense with the Water and Earth elements in their lives. They can put logs or branches of plants in their office or home, but they cannot put it in Water or Earth.

Sign of the Pig

People born under the sign of the Pig require the Fire element in their lives to bring good luck. They may place a ceramic tray, or other items made of clay in their home offices. Ceramic items are passed through fire for finishing.

About the Authors

In addition to her astrological knowledge, Alina A. Rubi has an abundant professional education; she holds certifications in Psychology, Hypnosis, Reiki, Bioenergetic Crystal Healing, Angelic Healing, Dream Interpretation and is a Spiritual Instructor. She possesses knowledge of Gemology, which she uses to program stones or minerals and turn them into powerful Amulets or Talismans of protection.

Ruby has a practical and purposeful character, which has allowed her to have a special and integrative vision of several worlds, facilitating solutions to specific problems. Alina writes the Monthly Horoscopes for the website of the American Association of Astrologers; you can read them at www.astrologers.com. At this moment she writes a weekly column in the newspaper El Nuevo Herald on spiritual topics, published every Friday in digital form and on Mondays in print. He also has a program and weekly Horoscope on the YouTube channel of this newspaper. Her Astrological Yearbook is published every year in the newspaper "Diario las Américas", under the column Rubi Astrologa.

Rubi has authored several articles on astrology for the monthly publication "Today's Astrologer", has taught classes in Astrology, Tarot, Palm Reading, Crystal Healing, and Esotericism. He has a weekly video on astrology topics on the New Herald's YouTube channel. She had her own Astrology program broadcast daily on Flamingo T.V., has been interviewed by several T.V. and radio programs, and every year she publishes her "Astrological Yearbook" with the horoscope sign by sign and other interesting mystical topics.

She is the author of the books "Rice and Beans for the Soul" Part I, II, and III a compilation of esoteric articles, published in English and Spanish languages, "Money for All Pockets", "Love for All Hearts", "Health for All Bodies", "Astrological Yearbook 2021", "Horoscope 2022", "Rituals and Spells for Success in 2022 Spells and Secrets",

"Astrology Classes", "Rituals and Charms 2024" and "Chinese Horoscope 2024" all available in seven languages.

She has her YouTube channel with topics on psychology, esotericism, and astrology, where you can enjoy videos on soul mates, reincarnation, body language, astral travel, evil eye, spells and many more topics.

Rubi is fluent in English and Spanish and combines all her talents and knowledge in her readings. She currently resides in Miami, Florida.

For more information you can visit the website www.esoterismomagia.com

Angeline A. Ruby is the daughter of Alina Ruby. Since she was a child, she has been interested in all esoteric subjects and has been practicing astrology and Kabbalah since she was four years old. She has knowledge of Tarot, Reiki, and Gemology. She is not only the author, but also the editor of all the books published by her and her mother.

For further information please contact her by email: rubiediciones29@gmail.com

Made in the USA
Las Vegas, NV
09 January 2024

84149532R00136